CORNWALL'S MARITIME HERITAGE

Alan Kittridge

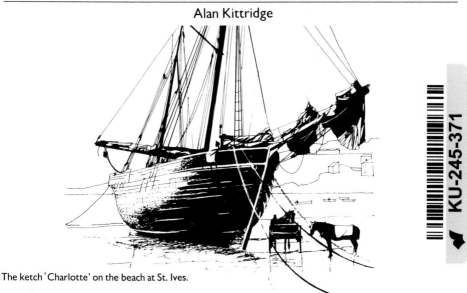

The ketch 'Charlotte' on the beach at St. Ives.

Evidence of Cornwall's maritime heritage is abundant. Indeed there are few towns or villages along the Cornish coast that do not owe their existence to the county's maritime trades, and few coves, beaches or rivers that have not witnessed some maritime activity.

The purpose of this book is to assist in identifying sites which have since returned to nature or subsequently been re-developed, to help interpret the surviving evidence and place the holiday haunts of today into their correct historical context.

Fishing and ferrying number amongst Cornwall's earliest maritime activities. The former established most of the county's picturesque fishing harbours, whilst the latter determined the route of many of its highways. Since at least the 11th century the export of tin represented an important factor in the development of Cornwall's trading ports and the promotion of general trade to the continent and the Mediterranean. During the Tudor and Stuart periods Cornwall found itself particularly well placed to benefit from trade with the colonies of the New World. But it is perhaps with the explosion of activity surrounding the Industrial Revolution during the 19th century that much of the county's current maritime landscape was created. Developments during this period included the building of docks, harbours and wharves to ship out the minerals, clay and fish, with which Cornwall was particularly well endowed.

Tourism in the county has been promoted ever since the Royal Albert Bridge at Saltash opened in 1859. Most of the county's notable resorts were developed during the latter half of the 19th century. As more leisure time becomes available and as more people retire to the Westcountry's kinder climate, more of Cornwall's past maritime facilities are utilised for pleasure. Today there are surely no remaining fishing coves that do not benefit from the holiday industry.

However, Cornwall's maritime importance is far from extinct. Both Fowey and Par remain busy in the china clay trade. Falmouth supports a large ship repair dock and other maritime trades. While Newlyn is one of the largest and busiest fishing harbours in the south of England.

TRADING PORTS AND HARBOURS

Centuries ago, when land transport was by horse and wagon on unsurfaced roads, water transport had many advantages as demonstrated by the 18th century development of inland canals. In a remote peninsula such as Cornwall it was the natural means of communication with the rest of the kingdom, as well as with more distant lands; few parts of the county were more than a dozen or so miles from the coast or from a navigable river.

The standard of living in the county was low, even by the levels of the day, and the population would have been largely self-sufficient until recent times.

Most ancient Cornish ports and harbours supported fishing fleets, the products of the sea being an important part of the Cornishman's diet since prehistoric times. With increasing industrial activity many of these old granite piers and jetties were extended and engaged in the export of minerals—tin, copper and, later, china clay, granite and slate. In most instances these activities went along with general local, continental—and even worldwide—import/export trade. Each harbour involved in general trading also supported its locally owned and, mostly, locally built merchant fleet. Such ports included Saltash, Looe, Fowey, Truro, Penryn, Falmouth, Penzance, St.Ives, Portreath, Padstow, Boscastle and, for a relatively brief period during the 19th & 20th centuries, Bude. The majority of these trading ports are located in the sheltered estuaries of the rivers Tamar, Looe, Fowey, Fal and Camel, or in bays protected from the prevailing

south westerly winds such as St.Austell Bay, Mounts Bay and St.Ives Bay.

Wherever ships called to take out tin, copper, clay, slate, agricultural goods or fish, they imported coal, timber, salt, limestone and general goods. Shipping agents were appointed to handle the trade and charter vessels when necessary. Falmouth, being strategically located as a safe anchorage at the entrance of the English Channel, became an important port for orders; as agents like G.C.Fox and W.Broad advised ships captains of their owners sailing instructions or fixed cargoes in other ports. Local merchant fleets were established, including the Stephens schooner fleet of Fowey, W.H.Lean of Falmouth, the Harveys of Hayle, D.W.Bain's schooners at Portreath, the fleet of Hitchens of St.Agnes, and the later tramping steamers of the Chellew Steam Navigation Company of Truro and Edward Hain of St Ives. Entire communities owned shares in ships, at times beyond all proportion to to the size of their harbour. Notable shipowning communities included Calstock on the River Tamar—over a dozen miles from the open sea; Par on St Austell Bay; Newquay—where well over 100 vessels were owned at the peak of activity; Padstow, which supported 27 shipowning concerns in 1823; Port Isaac on the north coast; and Bude—where a mainly agricultural community, remote from any major town, owned a considerable fleet until early in the 20th century.

Some of the earliest trading ports were established inland at or near the heads of navigation of rivers, rendering themselves less prone to raids from the sea and giving better access to the hinterland at a time when land transport was almost impractical for large loads. Such ports were Saltash on the River Tamar, Lostwithiel on the River Fowey, Tregony and Truro on the Fal Estuary, Helston on the River Cober and Lelant on the Hayle River. As the threat of attack diminished over the centuries, so too did the salt water in some of these places: the river at Lostwithiel silted badly; the tide which once reached Tregony began to recede during the middle ages; and Helston was isolated from the sea when the shingle of the Loe Bar formed a barrier across the Cober's mouth. The increas-

The harbour at Newquay.

Town Quay, Falmouth. Vessels include the schooner Mary Miller managed by C.W. Couch of Fowey, and the Kingsbridge built trading smack J.N.R. of 1893, which still survives at Weir Quay on the Devon bank of the River Tamar. The fishing vessels are former sailing pilchard drivers of Mounts Bay fitted out with engines.

ing size of ocean going shipping, particularly during the 19th century, further restricted navigation at inland ports like Truro and Wadebridge.

Ports and harbours at estuary mouths: Looe, Fowey, Falmouth and Padstow, and in sheltered coastal locations like Penzance and St.Ives, came to prominence and were well placed for the massive growth of maritime trade in the 19th century.

The southern coast of Cornwall is blessed with sheltered bays and drowned river valleys forming deep water sounds–the Carrick Roadstead in the Fal Estuary is acknowledged as one of the largest natural harbours in the world. Most of Cornwall's southern ports traded in tin during their early years. Penzance was a fishing harbour in Mounts Bay which became a coinage town and tin exporter during the 19th century. The port's general trade grew with successive harbour developments, which continued until the late 19th century.

The southern ports were particularly well placed for trade to the continent, both legal and otherwise! Privateering flourished at Fowey with the Mixtow family attacking French and

Spanish ships in the English Channel under Royal Licence. Smuggling–or 'free trading'–evaded heavy taxation and was undertaken between various Cornish harbours and, in particular, the Channel Islands.

Lostwithiel once was the most important of Cornwall's ancient trading ports, established initially as a port for Bodmin. Lostwithiel enjoyed a degree of security from its inland location but, like Truro, also suffered later from silting. The town of Fowey at the river's mouth was well placed to acquire Lostwithiel's trade. Fowey's trading prospects took an upward turn during the 19th century when china clay wharves were constructed immediately upstream from the town. The deep water harbour at Fowey lent itself to the establishment of merchant sailing fleets which engaged in the Newfoundland trade. This was based on carrying salted fish to the Mediterranean and salt back across to the small settlements on the coast of Newfoundland which survived by fishing for the plentiful cod in those waters. The largest fleet of schooners was owned by John Stephens and, quite typically, his small, fast and sea-worthy vessels were well suited to the salt

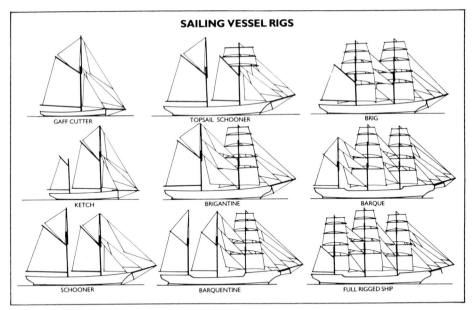

SAILING VESSEL RIGS

GAFF CUTTER   TOPSAIL SCHOONER   BRIG

KETCH   BRIGANTINE   BARQUE

SCHOONER   BARQUENTINE   FULL RIGGED SHIP

fish trade. Like the fast schooners of the south Devon ports–particularly Salcombe–used in the fruit trade from the Azores and Mediterranean, all benefited from the local builders' experience gained by an earlier need to outsail the Revenue cutters!.

By the beginning of this century even these small fleets were feeling considerable economic pressures from the introduction of steam power and iron construction. Much trade, even locally, was being lost to shipping which was no longer so dependent on the weather and which carried larger cargoes, quicker than even the best west country schooner. These new vessels required a different kind of boatyard for their building and a much greater investment; with a

Fowey Harbour with Polruan on the left.

few exceptions neither of these was available in Cornwall. The ageing sailing vessels hung on to some trade until the first world war, where the need for speed, or the value of the cargo did not justify the change to steam. With auxiliary engines fitted, others continued to work, their longevity a tribute to the local shipwrights; right up to the early 1960s, for instance, much of the County Council's roadstone was carried by motorised sailing ketches.

The southern ports were also convenient for shipping plying to the Baltic, the Mediterranean and the Atlantic. After its early history as a Post Office Packet station for the Iberian Peninsula, the Caribbean, and North Atlantic, Falmouth was particularly well placed to profit from its role as the port for orders for ships in the English Channel, a role which faded when ship to shore radio communications were established during the early years of this century.

The ancient port of Looe–or more precisely East and West Looe, as the two sides of the harbour were once separate boroughs–has long supported a fishing fleet and once exported minerals from the Caradon mining district. General trading was given a boost in the 1820's when the Liskeard & Looe Union Canal was built, primarily to improve communication between Looe and the mining district.

The Quay, West Looe with the trading ketch Hope alongside and fishing luggers drying their sails.

The geography of Cornwall's north coast did not lend itself to the establishment of large trading ports. The one substantial estuary of the River Camel is obstructed by sandbanks, formed by the dual action of tide and river flow.

The canal and sea lock at Bude. A group of trading vessels await the tide in the shelter of the breakwater. The sand tramway is on the right.

The port of Padstow and the river quays at Wadebridge enjoyed a period of success in the 19th century. But a decline in their mineral trade coupled with unfavourable navigation conditions has prevented any revival of the river's general trade.

St.Ives is most closely associated with the fishing industry, but the port attracted considerable general trade, restricted however to beach landing, albeit protected by Smeaton;s pier since 1770.

A succession of man made harbours were built at Hayle, Portreath, St.Agnes, Newquay and Bude to cater initially for the mining, quarrying and agricultural industries. In the absence of any substantial natural alternative, these harbours also attracted general trade.

Sheltered sandy coves along the north coast lent themselves to potentially hazardous beach trading. Small coastal schooners, ketches and smacks came in to 'take the beach' as the tide receded. Vessels were developed with flatter hulls similar to the river barges, better suited for standing on a beach than for seaworthyness and speed on the open sea. Three of these inlets, Port Isaac, Port Gaverne and Boscastle exported Delabole slate and established their own small fleets of merchant vessels, trading mainly in the Irish Sea and the Bristol Channel.

FISHING

There is hardly a beach, cove or stretch of river bank along the entire coastline that has not at some stage figured in the long story of fishing in Cornwall.

Foremost in the fisherman's calendar was the pilchard season which began around July and lasted for about four months. This modestly-sized, oily fish, the adult of the sardine, was responsible for the development of virtually all of Cornwall's picturesque fishing villages and coves; their economic survival depended on the pilchard until they were discovered by the 19th and 20th century visitors.

Smoked, pickled or (exclusively by the 19th century) salted, pilchards found an inexhaustable market in Mediterranean countries, particularly during the Lenten fasts of Catholics. Pilchards numbering in millions raced towards the Cornish coast each year. Huge shoals darkened the water and obligingly divided at Lands End to feed Sennen, St.Ives and the northern coast, while the southern shoals were gathered in Mounts Bay, off the Lizard, Falmouth Bay, St.Austell Bay, Looe and Cawsand Bay. This pilchard fishery remained an almost entirely Cornish phenomenon.

Shovelling pilchards into carts at Sennen Cove.

Complete shoals numbering at times 200 hogsheads (2500–3000 pilchards per hogshead) were taken in a day. Shoals were encircled by seine nets, hauled into shallow 'shoal' water and anchored. Pilchard seining was undertaken by seine companies with names such as the Unity Seine, the Poor Man's Adventure Seine, Bolitho

Lifting pilchards from the seine net with tuck baskets.

Western Seine and the Mullion Seine. Each seine usually had three boats, two nets and fish cellars, or 'palaces', ashore. The first boat was the low and broad *seine boat*, up to 40ft. in length. It was six oared, crewed by seven or eight men and carried the seine net which was shot around the shoal. The second boat was the *follower*, variously corrupted around the coast as *follier*, *vollier* or *volyer*, which carried the stop or tuck net, used to lift the fish from the water. Pilchards were then transferred to gurries (barrows) or maunds (baskets) in which they were carried ashore to the bulking house. The third boat was the *lurker*, *lurcher* or *larker*, a smaller, faster boat of four oars which carried the Master Seiner, who directed the operation. A cliff top look out sometimes directed the seines with semaphore signals.

At St.Ives there was room for 20 seines to be worked at any one time. By 1870 there were over 280 seine companies registered in this port alone! Each seine was allocated a 'stem' to work, while signals on Porthminster Beach notified change over times. Seining was a rich mans fishery, during the 19th century each company cost about £1000 to establish.

Once ashore in the curing cellars or palaces, the pilchards were bulked or balked—salted in layers, packed heads out and tails towards the centre. The resulting pilchard oil which drained off was sold separately. Fishing families salted about 1500-2000 fish for their own consumption during the winter.

By 1870 there were 379 seines in Cornwall divided as follows:

St.Ives	285
Mounts Bay	23
Mevagissey	10
Newquay	9
St Mawes	9
others	43

Towards the end of the 19th century the pilchard shoals inexplicably began to desert the Cornish coast. Already by the 1850's Cornwall's drift fishery had gained the ascendancy over the seine fishery. In 1870 there were 635 driving boats registered:

Mounts Bay	339
Newlyn	130
Mousehole	105
Porthleven	104
St.Ives	186
Mevagissey	61
Looe	22
others, in 7 other ports	37

Before the 17th century drift nets had been used to catch pilchards and other fish further offshore. A long standing feud developed, the seiners claiming that the driving boats were breaking up the shoals before the seines could enclose them. The Long Parliament of the Restoration restricted the use of drift nets to three miles offshore from June to November inclusive.

Whilst ownership of a seine company represented a considerable investment, a driving boat, with nets, cost around £250, in the early 19th century. Builders like William Paynter of St.Ives, Blewett of Newlyn, James Wills of Penzance and Bowden or Kitto of Porthleven, built pilchard drivers–lug sailed, half decked, about 28ft. long–and mackerel drivers–two masted luggers, fully decked and up to 50ft. in length. Luggers built in south east Cornwall, from Mevagissey to Looe, had square transoms. St.Ives, Penzance and Newlyn boats had a sharp stem to save space in crowded harbours. While those of Porthleven had a rounded counter stern to give protection from the following seas encountered on the east side of Mounts Bay. St.Ives boats had rounder bilges, to take the ground in the drying harbour. Mounts Bay boats, inside their better protected harbours used wooden legs when lying on the beach. At Polperro a smaller boat was developed, gaff

Newlyn's original pier within the subsequently enlarged harbour.

rigged but without a boom. At Mevagissey similar small boats were called Toshers.

The mackerel season lasted from January to June. The drift fleet worked off the Eddystone and the Isles of Scilly, sailing out into the Atlantic west of Wolf Rock during the main season. From June to August herring were fished in the Irish and North Seas followed by the pilchard season and handlining for hake—which followed the pilchard shoals.

In addition to the seine and drift fleets, crabbing boats around the entire coast set pots offshore. The Sennen Cove crabber a two masted, lug sailed boat about 20ft. long, was one example of a fishing craft developed locally to suit the environment of the particular harbour or cove. At Saltash on the Tamar, in the Carrick Roadstead and on the Helford River, oyster beds were dredged. The Falmouth working boat, a smack rigged gaffer, was developed to work the oyster beds. Even today a small number of these distinctive craft remain amongst the last working sailing craft in the country, powered vessels being prohibited over the oyster beds. A few examples of wooden hulled working boats survive, one of the oldest being the yellow hulled *Victory*. Moulds have been taken off these vessels to produce a growing number of glass fibre versions which race regularly in the Carrick Roads.

Once Cornwall's railways were linked to the mainline from London in 1859, the railway opened up new, larger markets. 'Foreign' fleets were attracted to the Cornish fishing grounds, including trawlers from Plymouth, Brixham and the East Coast. Penzance became the main Cornish harbour for the East Coast fleet.

The drift fleet fell into decline during the early 20th century. In 1920 the last pilchard driver was fitted out with engines at Newlyn. Just one example of a Cornish driving boat has survived, the *Barnabas*, a mackerel driver, built in St.Ives in 1881, is maintained in sailing condition by the Cornish Friends of the Maritime Trust.

The change of port authorities can be noted by the registration port initials painted on the fishing boats: FY (Fowey); FH (Falmouth); PZ (Penzance); SS (St.Ives); and PW (Padstow). In addition to this list is PH (Plymouth), which covers the south east Cornish coast from the Tamar to Seaton Bay.

Fishing remains an important Cornish industry, as can be seen by the extensive improvements which have been made in Newlyn with a new and often crowded jetty. The industry has changed out of all recognition in recent years; foreign factory-ships are to be seen off-shore, and with modern technological developments extensive over-fishing of many species has resulted. Apparently illogical regulations are imposed with political directives and controls from Whitehall and Brussels and these often seem to do no more than result in dead fish being thrown back into the sea, once a 'quota' has been reached.

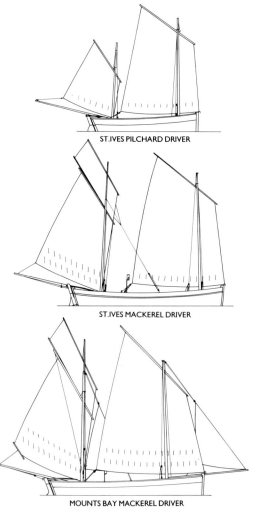

ST.IVES PILCHARD DRIVER

ST.IVES MACKEREL DRIVER

MOUNTS BAY MACKEREL DRIVER

Fishing luggers at the quay, East Looe.

SMUGGLING

The involvement with smuggling in Cornwall has been romanticised by a succession of popular novelists and, perhaps most extremely, by the county's tourist trade. Rather ludicrous Treasure Island-like characters are credited with Cornwall's smuggling heritage, their piratical faces adorning cafe signs and amusement arcades. The truth about this illegal activity however is probably stranger than the fiction.

Smuggling became an economic necessity for many in Cornwall, particularly after a Salt Duty was introduced during the late 17th century. Salt from the continent was used for curing pilchards. This was one of the mainstays of the Cornish fishing industry and a major source of winter food throughout the county. The duty sometimes could amount to about half of the fishermens' meagre income! Therefore salt was smuggled in to avoid paying the tax. It is probably more correct to say that salt was imported into isolated fishing villages and coves as before, but the cargoes remained undeclared to the authorities. However, the opportunity was also taken to trade in other heavily taxed, less essential commodities such as wine, spirits, tea and tobacco. The higher the import tariffs were raised, the more lucrative became the profit for smugglers. This activity, known as 'free trading', was viewed with sympathy by the local population, and many members of the local community, up to and including the local gentry, often colluded in the trade.

In Polperro, Zephaniah Job was entrusted by the free traders with their finances; Job meticulously maintained their accounts and himself backed various smuggling ventures, later establishing his own note-issuing bank. Capt. James Dunn of Mevagissey was a wealthy master mariner, shipbuilder, shipowner and smuggler and reputedly the village was largely rebuilt from the proceeds of the free trade.

Merchants in Guernsey specialised in supplying goods to the Cornish free traders. One of the most powerful suppliers was Carteret Priaulx & Co., once the largest commercial trading house in Guernsey. The company's agents openly toured Cornwall to tout for business. Government observers recorded cargoes and ships names at the quayside in Guernsey, but could only gain a smuggling conviction if they were caught in the act of landing goods illegally in England. Customs officials had few resources at their disposal and received little or no assistance from the local population. In Fowey, in 1835, five men charged with being amongst some 100 smugglers who had fought Preventive men, were acquitted after Crown jury decided that the sticks with which they had been armed were not offensive weapons!

Favoured destinations for landing smuggled goods included Mounts Bay, the Fal Estuary, Portloe and Looe, but Cawsand, Polperro and Mevagissey remained the chief strongholds of the free trade.

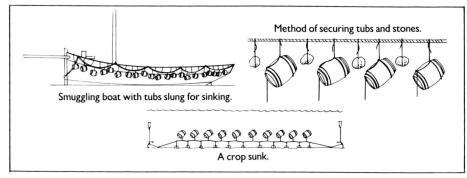

Method of securing tubs and stones.

Smuggling boat with tubs slung for sinking.

A crop sunk.

Eight oared volyer boats from the pilchard seines were favoured for landing goods. The principal cross channel smuggling craft were cutters and sloops, which were fast and could easily be beached in secluded coves. The free traders' boats were invariably faster than the Government craft, while the smugglers possessed an intimate knowledge of their local waters. In the 1770's it was estimated that some 469,000 gallons of brandy and 350,000 pounds of tea were being smuggled into the country annually.

During the latter half of the 18th century the Government began to take steps to redress the balance. An anti-smuggling Act of 1779 declared that ships under 200 tons, carrying illegal packages, would be forfeit. Between 1786 and 1815, 81 Fowey vessels were seized. Following a later Act, cutters were forfeit as smuggling craft unless they were square rigged, (fore and aft rigged vessels could sail very close to the wind, outrunning larger, but square rigged government ships) or if they were fitted with a bowsprit larger than two thirds of the boat's length. Unless square rigged, or a sloop with a standing bowsprit, no vessel of any kind was to be clinker built, but such craft were still built—and subsequently seized. In 1784 fast, long sailing ships, with a length more than 3½ times their breadth, were banned unless licenced. Despite all these regulation, many 'illegal' vessels continued to be built, especially in Mevagissey and Fowey and, surprisingly, were even entered into the official Port register!

Some 29 vessels at this time were known by the authorities to be engaged in smuggling, but unlike free traders in the south east, most of the Cornishmen were armed. Around 300 seamen were engaged in the trade in Cornwall, backed up by a far larger number of landsmen. In 1809 the Preventive Water Guard was formed, equipped with galleys and gigs. They not only patrolled inshore along the free trader's coast, but additionally checked on the activity of the Revenue cutters further offshore. In 1816 the Revenue cutters were transferred to the jurisdiction of the Royal Navy. Ashore, Riding Officers patrolled the coast, with powers of search up to 10 miles inland. Violent clashes occurred, so an 'outside' armed and mounted force, the Inniskillen Dragoons, were billeted in Truro. In 1822 the Preventive Water Guard, Revenue cutters and Riding Officers were amalgamated to form the Coastguard. After 1841 the Customs House staff in the Port of Fowey—with jurisdiction over Mevagissey and Polperro—included: a Surveyor, Controller, Collector, three Officers, a Land Waiter (to keep watch over vessels in the harbour whereas a Tide Waiter could board a ship before it had anchored), three Salt Officers, a Searcher of Salt, and an Excise Officer. In addition, the Customs House received frequent calls from Riding Officers and cutters of the Coastguard.

An Act of 1805 extended the law against smuggling to 100 leagues from the mainland, the new area deliberately included the Channel Islands. No sooner was a Customs House established on the island, than the French port of Roscoff was declared a free port to win the trade. But reductions in taxes, coupled with increased law enforcement, began to render the trade less attractive. By 1815 the 'acceptable' face of the old free trade was fading. Although old habits died slowly, particularly in south east Cornwall, smuggling or free trading had ceased to pose a significant problem by the second half of the 19th century.

THE MINERAL QUAYS

Calstock Quay and the quayside mineral railway sidings. On the viaduct is the wagon hoist which replaced the original incline down to the quay.

Just as Cornwall's fishing heritage is evidenced today by the existence of numerous coastal villages, so too can the county's mining and quarrying industries be witnessed by dozens of ruined mine engine houses, spoil tips and vast man made craters.

Cornwall was particularly well endowed with the largest deposits of tin and copper ore in Europe. Tin ore has been excavated in the county since prehistoric times and the industry continues today. In the 19th century Cornwall was the most important source of copper ore in the world. Cornish granite quarries provided the raw materials prestigious engineering works including the building of the Chelsea Embankment, London Bridge, Dover Harbour improvements, Portland Naval Base and two consecutive Eddystone Lighthouses. Blue elvan roadstones and various granite chippings were won both from inland quarries and from spectacular cliff sites around the coast, while in north Cornwall a vast crater continues to offer up Delabole slate. Since the beginning of the last century, of increasing importance has been china clay, the majority coming from the area around St Austell.

It has been calculated that during the last century about 20,000,000 tons of copper ore, tin and china clay went away from Cornish ports, a not inconsiderable quantity, when it is remembered that most of this was carried on sailing ships with a capacity of 100 or 200 tons. Of this quantity, until about 1860, copper predominated, this being sent away as ore for smelting in south Wales, mostly in the Swansea valley. Returning ships carried coal which the deepening mines required for their steam pumping engines. As copper declined in the last decades of the century, so china clay increased in production to replace the metals as major cargoes. All of these minerals and stones were exported by sea from docks, jetties and beaches, bound in the main for British and continental ports. The earliest trade in tin, to the mediterranean, certainly dates back 2000 years.

Foremost amongst Cornwall's ancient ports were Truro, Lostwithiel and Saltash, each of which grew in importance from the export of tin. Later, as Lostwithiel and Saltash (exporting tin from Dartmoor) declined, the ports of Fowey and Penzance grew in stature.

Tin and copper ore, granite and slate were laboriously transported to the nearest navigable point by packhorse. Such quays and landing places as were available were primarily fishing harbours: Boscastle with slate and mineral ores from Bodmin Moor; St Ives and Penzance with tin and copper from Penwith and Looe, exporting tin and copper from Caradon. Long established river landings included Padstow and Wadebridge on the River Camel with minerals and stone from Bodmin Moor; Gweek, on the Helford River served Helston and local mines and quarries; Truro, Roundwood Quay, Pill Creek and Penryn on the Fal Estuary took minerals and stone from the Carnon Valley and Gwennap; on the River Tamar, Cotehele and Calstock exported minerals and stone from Gunnislake and the Tamar Valley mines; Forder and St German's Quay on the St German's River had extensive trade in stone from numerous local quarries. Other landing places included the extensive sand banks off Par taking cargoes of minerals and stone from the Luxulyan Valley, and the north Cornish 'Porths' of Port Isaac and Port Gaverne which exported Delabole slate.

In the 18th and 19th centuries the industrial revolution produced an explosion of activity in Cornwall's mineral industries, and the county strived to satisfy the industrial world's insatiable demand for raw materials. A series of developments were undertaken to improve communications and harbour facilities.

In 1760 a pier was constructed at Portreath to improve the shipment of minerals; a basin was added in 1800 and nine years later the Poldice Tramroad was built to link the harbour with the mining district around Redruth. Improvements continued throughout the 19th century. There was a very long and narrow harbour entrance which restricted the size of ships. But the port served its purpose, exporting copper ore to Swansea for smelting and importing Welsh coal to fire the beam engines which drained the mines and powered other machinery.

A second development along the north coast was the establishment of a harbour in Trevaunance Cove, after several failed attempts. Named St Agnes Harbour, it served the St Agnes mining district. Clinging to the shore below cliffs, this exposed little harbour suffered constantly from gale damage. Once it had fallen out of use early in the 20th century, the sea quickly demolished the protecting piers.

The third and most significant development on the north coast followed the establishment of a foundry by John Harvey in the Hayle River estuary during 1779. Harvey's foundry become world famous for its pumping engines and other mining machinery. In 1818-1819 the foundry company improved navigation of the Hayle River and built a quay for vessels of up to 150 tons to come alongside the Company's works. Opposition was forthcoming from the nearby Copperhouse Company, which built their own Copperhouse Quay. Both companies engaged in foundry work, shipped ore for smelting in South Wales and imported coal and timber for the mines, although Harvey's competitor failed in the 1860s. Harvey's also owned their own merchant fleet and after 1831 ran a steam packet service to Bristol—later linking with the new, Great Western Railway from London.

The Hayle quays at the turn of the century.

Following a decline in the mining boom during the second half of the 19th century, Harvey's concentrated on shipbuilding and foundry work, being the only significant builder of iron ships in Cornwall. The foundry and shipyard closed in 1904, although the name survived until recent years, trading as builders merchants.

Although lacking natural sites for harbour development, the north Cornwall coast attracted proposals because of its proximity to the smelting works and coal mines of South Wales, whilst avoiding the longer and more hazardous alternative of a voyage around Land's End.

However, the majority of Cornwall's maritime trade was on the south coast, with many sheltered potential locations for quays and, generally, shorter and easier transport from the mines to navigable water.

The quay at Penryn.

The S.S. Islesman entering Portreath.

Porthoustock with the loading jetties of the West of England Roadstone Company on the right.

For instance, in 1826, a major mineral quay development was undertaken, not on an exposed coastal site, but tucked away in what today is a quiet backwater of the Fal Estuary.

In 1826 the Redruth & Chasewater Railway Company selected a waterside site at Devoran, near the head of Restronguet Creek, to serve as terminus and wharves for its 4ft, gauge mineral tramway which ran through the Redruth, Gwennap, St Day and Carnon Valley mining districts. Restronguet Creek already supported a smelting works at Point and a foundry at Perranarworthal. As the new wharves developed they drew trade away from the older mineral quays at nearby Roundwood Quay and Pill Creek. Sail traders and steamships visited Devoran's wharves, which grew to a considerable size. Silting always proved a problem, only partially solved by a reservoir sluice which scoured the channel, and paddle tugs which assisted the merchant ships. However, the quays survived the test of time, only falling into disrepair after closure of the railway in 1915.

The improvement in the construction of roads, particularly following the introduction of motor transport, called for the supply of stone chippings. One of the most spectacular of these roadstone quarries is at Porthoustock, where the cliff itself is being quarried away. River barges collected their cargoes of stone at Porthoustock by sailing under the loading shute jetties, which still dominate the shoreline. One of the main destinations on the Fal Estuary was Cornwall County Council's Highways depot at Tresillian, the highest navigable point on the estuary. River barges continued in this trade for many years after the Second World War. Similar quarries at Penlee in Mounts Bay were served by a narrow gauge railway, carrying the stone to Newlyn's South Pier. St Ives' West Pier was similarly given over to serve nearby quarries.

Another stronghold of the roadstone trade was the estuary of the River Lynher and River Tiddy in east Cornwall where, well into the second half of this century, Thames spritsail barges and Dutch motor coasters were numbered amongst the vessels plying these idyllic waters to take out stone from Poldrissick, Treluggan and Forder Quays.

THE CHINA CLAY PORTS

William Cookworthy, a Plymouth chemist, searched geologically-suitable areas in the west country for the materials needed in the production of Chinese-style porcelain, the manufacture of which had remained a secret for centuries. He discovered deposits of Kaolin or china-clay, as it became known, in west Cornwall and then, in the St Austell district, he not only discovered a suitable supply, but seemingly inexhaustable deposits of the finest china clay in the world. By the 1780s he had established his own porcelain manufactory in Plymouth. The mining and quarrying of this clay was to transform the landscape of central Cornwall and initiate the development of some of the most substantial and longest lasting of all Cornwall's harbours built during the Industrial Revolution.

Ships took china clay out from the beaches at Porthpean, Pentewan, West Polmear and Par, for St Austell Bay had no natural harbour. But such landings were severely disrupted by storms, especially during the winter months. By 1800 production had reached 2000 tons a year and with an ever increasing demand from the Staffordshire potteries for china clay, a series of harbour developments in St Austell Bay resulted.

As the result of three ships being lost at West Polmear in 1790, the local landowner, Charles Rashleigh, began the construction of a pier the

Par Harbour in the 1950's

next year. Based on the engineer John Smeaton's concept, during the next seven years the excavation of an inner basin took place, protected by lock gates and an outer basin. Warehouses and dwellings, hotel, ropewalk, fish cellars and a boat-building yard completed the new community, the population of which increased from 9 to 900 during the next decade. West Polmear became Charlestown.

A quarter of a century later a second harbour development was nearing completion. Since 1744 the Hawkins family had established harbour facilities at Pentewan, about three miles south of Charlestown, near the mouth of the St Austell River. By the turn of the century these harbour works were derelict and shipping had reverted to beach landings. In 1817 Sir Charles

CHINA CLAY PROCESSING AND LOADING ARRANGEMENT AT CHARLESTOWN

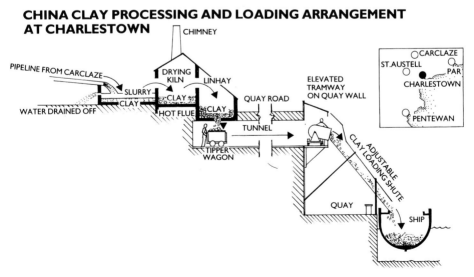

Hawkins entered into an agreement for the construction of a new harbour on the site. The work was completed in 1826 and linked to St Austell by a horse tramway three years later. The bulk of the china clay traffic was diverted through the streets of St Austell to reach the new harbours. By 1830 the town had become seriously congested with clay wagons. A third harbour scheme was promoted in St Austell Bay. Although initially intended to export granite and copper ore, Par Harbour later outgrew its two neighbours in the china clay trade. This artificial harbour was promoted and financed by Joseph Thomas Austen of Fowey, to serve his Luxulyan Valley quarries and Fowey Consols mine. Construction work commenced in 1829 on the open beach at Par. By 1840 a 1200ft breakwater and pier enclosed 35 acres. A three mile stretch of the Luxulyan River, from Par to Pontsmill, was canalised. From the canal terminus an incline plane served Fowey Consols mine, while a seven mile tramroad to the granite quarries on Molinnis Moors reached the north east edge of the china clay district.

Contemporary with the Par development was a scheme to provide harbour facilities at Newquay, (on the north coast) which was then noth-

ing more than a small fishing hamlet, the 'New' quay dating from the 16th century. In 1833 Richard Lomax completed work on the harbour piers which enclosed an area of four acres and was accessible to vessels up to 700 tons at all states of the tide. In 1838 Joseph Thomas. Treffry (Austen had changed his name to that of his mother's, co-heiress of the Treffrys of Fowey) purchased Newquay Harbour from Lomax, further extended it and, in 1844, obtained an Act of Parliament to build a railway from Newquay into the china clay district.

The relative importance to the china clay trade of these harbours, might be gauged by noting the clay shipments from each in 1858:

Charlestown/Pentewan	64,845 tons
Par	15,154 tons
Newquay	2,788 tons
Truro	150 tons
Padstow	25 tons
others	150 tons

Pentewan was soon struggling to survive. The valleys of the St Austell River and its tributaries passed through stream works and the china clay district, silt from which was choking the harbour entrance adjacent to the mouth of the river.

All of the above ventures were artificial har-

Pentewan Harbour.

bours, constructed as near as possible to the clay and mining districts. The nearest natural harbour was the deep water estuary of the Fowey River and the introduction of steam railways in the mid 19th century finally rendered Fowey's vast natural resource within reach of the mineral and clay districts. In Caffa Mill Pill, immediately upstream from Fowey, J.T.Treffry had built a small dock because, prior to his Par scheme, he had contemplated building a railway from his mines to Carn Point, near Caffa Mill Pill. A railway line was again projected in 1861 and eventually built and opened by the Cornwall Railway in 1869. Five years later the Cornwall Minerals Railway, in connection with the Cornish Iron Mining Corporation, opened a line from Par to Fowey. Its primary objective was to ship an expected 1000 tons of iron ore per day from Fowey Harbour. These two railways also provided Fowey with a direct connection to the china clay district.

The iron ore traffic failed to materialise, but the Cornwall Minerals Railway survived on the clay trade and introduced hydraulic wagon tipping frames, for loading clay into the ships' holds. The Great Western Railway took over in 1876 and developed the facilities at Fowey, especially after the turn of the century.

In the last quarter of the 19th century exports from Fowey, Par and Charlestown exceeded all other clay ports by a huge margin.

Clay shipped in 1885:

Fowey	114,403 tons
Par	86,325 tons
Charlestown	59,690 tons
Pentewan	24,960 tons
Newquay	4,152 tons
Penzance	1,570 tons
Padstow/Wadebridge	1,475 tons
Penryn	1,024 tons
Porthleven	860 tons
Hayle	390 tons

Fowey's deep water berths served ocean going shipping from the United States, Canada, Russia etc. Par and Charlestown catered for smaller vessels in the coastal and Home Trades—Germany, Netherlands, Belgium, France.

Pentewan's silting problems continued. In 1877 steam locomotives were introduced on the harbour's mineral line, greatly improving communication with St Austell. But horse drawn wagons, in even greater numbers, still needed to negotiate St Austell's streets to reach the railway's terminus, as they also had to for Charlestown. Silting of the harbour mouth remained a major problem, attempts at curing the silting generally failed, or even made matters worse. Pentewan continued in slow decline until the railway equipment was requisitioned during the first world war. The harbour changed hands in 1918 and a new trade flourished briefly—the supply of building sand, for which the silt clogging the harbour proved admirable! The last clay cargo left the harbour in 1929—although this was something of a 'one off' event. The last trading vessels called in 1940 for cargoes of cement or concrete blocks.

The trade at Charlestown continued steadily despite its disadvantages in horse wagon days, and the severe limit to shipping resulting from the constricted entrance. New lock gates were fitted in 1971. The number of vessels visiting the harbour in 1980 was 144, taking out 61,000 tons of clay, mostly for the independent Goonvean and Rostowrack China Clay Co, a figure little changed since 1885. The harbour and village remained in the ownership of one family for about 160 years, and little has changed in that time, although following the sale of Charlestown in 1986 some development is likely to take place. The unique character of the centre of the village and harbour should be protected at all costs.

Clay now arrives by road or rail or in liquid form by pipeline, at Par which remains the main harbour for small European motor coasters, while Fowey can handle ships of about 12,000 tons, and in 1986 handled 1.6 million tons of cargo, almost all of it china clay.

A clay ship loading at the clay jetties on the River Fowey.

RIVER QUAYS AND FERRIES

A river barge at Percuil with two crewmen working the winch. The building behind is a manure store. On the far left is the Percuil Ferry.

It is perhaps with its fishing villages and rugged coastline that Cornwall's maritime heritage is most closely associated, but at intervals the granite cliffs break rank and the sea spills inland to fill the estuaries of the Tamar, Looe, Fowey, Fal, Helford and Camel Rivers. Prior to the advent of railways such tidal estuaries were invaluable to the trade and development of their waterside communities. A glance at the map of Cornwall offers evidence of this importance. Saltash, Looe, Fowey, Lostwithiel, Falmouth, Penryn, Truro, Padstow and Wadebridge each owe their existence to the river estuary upon which they grew. The coastal and deep sea trades which such ports supported are described elsewhere in this book.

Upon each of Cornwall's navigable estuaries there evolved local 'inside' trades, ranging from simple drifting lighters on the River Camel, to large sailing barge fleets on the Rivers Tamar and Fal. Small rowing boat ferries provided passage across the narrower stretches of river. Large steamboat fleets offered passenger communication between a number of river quays; maritime lorries and buses as it were, usually working to the very limit of salt water to serve the estuarine communities and industries of Cornwall.

The river traffic varied on each estuary, dependent upon the landbased industries, size of population and the nature of the estuary itself. In the Tamar valley an ideal environment for fruit and vegetable growing was matched at the river's mouth by the 'Three Towns' of Plymouth, Devonport and Stonehouse–the largest centre of population on the south coast of England. In addition, the Tamar Valley became

A river barge sailing past the King Harry Ferry on the River Fal.

an area of intense industrial activity. Thus there grew a large fleet of river barges, to carry manure and supplies up-river and agricultural and industrial produce down. In the Hamoaze, at the mouth of the Tamar, the Royal Dockyard was established at Devonport, offering jobs to the east Cornwall communities of Saltash, Torpoint and Millbrook. Passage across the Hamoaze was readily provided by the likes of the Saltash & St Germans Steamboat Co Ltd, the Torpoint Steam Launch Co Ltd, the Millbrook Steamboat Company and many others.

On the Tamar and Fal estuaries a large number of river barges worked the quiet backwaters to lonely quays. Many of these barges were owned and manned by the same agricultural communities they were built to serve. Inside barges were usually smack rigged, carrying a huge mainsail and topsail to catch the slightest breeze in the sheltered estuaries. When the elements conspired against the bargeman, long sweeps (oars) or quant poles (like punting poles) were brought into use. Fully laden these barges could sail with just two inches of freeboard. They had very strong hulls for taking the ground at uneven mud berths. Barge builders

included Emmanuel Crocker of Gunnislake, James Goss of Calstock, George Westcott and George Fisher of Saltash, Charles Burt of Falmouth, William Scoble and John Davies of Malpas and Charles Dyer of Sunny Corner, Truro. In addition to its river barges, the Port of Truro also supported a fleet of river lighters. These served ships with too deep a draught to reach Truro fully laden. River barges called at farm quays such as Buttspill, Terrace Meadows and Collogget on the Tamar estuary, and Polingey, Cowlands and Trewince on the Fal. Agricultural trade was also established at river ferry crossings such as Halton Quay, Cargreen, or Percuil, owing in the main to their long established accessability from both the river and the surrounding farmland.

Ferries have long crossed Cornwall's rivers at convenient points. The right to operate the earliest ferries was granted to respective landowners by the sovereign of the day. The Saltash Ferry was owned by the Valletort family after the Norman Conquest. In the 14th century it was bestowed to the Mayor and Burgesses of Saltash. The Earls of Mount Edgcumbe maintained the Cremyll Ferry until they sold the rights in 1946. The Flushing Ferry, in Falmouth

The Saltash floating bridge or chain ferry No.3, built by Willoughby's of Millbay, Stonehouse in 1891. The river barge is the Calstock owned Silver Spray, built by C. F. Williams of Stonehouse in 1880.

The preserved Tamar barge Shamrock off Cotehele Quay. *Richard Clammer*

Harbour, was granted by Charles II to Sir Peter Killigrew in 1660. On the Helford River, the Manor of Merthen held the rights to the Helford Ferry. The Percuil Ferry on the Fal Estuary was an example of an ecclesiastical ferry, being owned by the Bishops of Sherborne until it passed to the Bishop of Exeter in the 10th century and the Church Commissioners in 1835. On the River Camel the Padstow-Rock ferry dates back to the creation of the Duchy in 1337.

Some ancient ferries offered an indispensable river crossing on the main routes through the county. Their importance can be judged by the number which still operate. The Cremyll Ferry, at the mouth of the Tamar has operated since 'time immemorial' and still provides a year round ferry crossing. The Saltash Ferry closed in 1961, replaced by the suspension bridge. On the Fowey River both the Polruan pedestrian ferry and the Bodinnick vehicular ferry date back to the 1300s and still operate year round. Two ancient crossings remain on the Fal, the Flushing pedestrian ferry and the King Harry vehicular ferry.

Communities and other convenient crossing places have also been served periodically by ferries or steamer services which were established as circumstances demanded. The Rumleigh ferry on the Tamar linked Calstock and the Okel Tor Mine to Gawton Mine and Rumleigh Brickworks on the Bere Alston peninsula. The

Mylor-Greatwood ferry on the Fal estuary survived for as long as the Naval Dockyard at Mylor existed. On the River Gannel, the Fern Pit and Crantock ferries were established in the 19th century to serve visitors wishing to cross the river when the tide was in. Saltash, Torpoint and Millbrook steamboat services provided important services on the Hamoaze, gradually fading out with the growth of motor transport. Some major crossings which were established in the 18th and 19th centuries remain important today. The Torpoint ferry is by far the largest and busiest vehicular river ferry operating in Britain and the St Mawes passenger boat service, which links the one time fishing village to Falmouth, is as busy today as it ever was.

The Millbrook — Devonport steamer Lady Ernestine.

The Falmouth tug-tender Penguin.

Whilst paddle steamers reigned supreme on the River Tamar market boat and river packet services, the steamers of the River Fal were almost all tug-like, screw steamers. In addition to maintaining river services on the Fal, these rugged steamers of the River Fal Steamship Co Ltd and the St Mawes Steam Tug & Passenger Co Ltd also provided the opportunity to view the Cornish coast between Penzance and Plymouth. Motor road transport eventually killed off the barge trade and many ferries. The river steamer services have largely evolved into river-trip boats which, in Millbrook, base for the Tamar services, are still the largest source of employment in the village.

The Bodinnick Ferry c.1920.

The crew and owners of the Tamar paddle steamer Hibernia in 1904.

BEACH TRADING

There are not many coves or beaches along the Cornish coast that have not witnessed some maritime activity. Fishing and trading vessels utilised many such places which had reasonable access from the land. The coast is littered with these trading places or 'Porths', where small sailing vessels came in, and were run aground at high tide. As the tide ebbed, they could be unloaded ready to float off on the next high tide preferably with the help of a wind off the land!Some later developed into harbours, but the beaching of small boats continues at smaller fishing coves like Penberth, where a windlass survives which formerly hauled boats up the steep beach to safety.

Three trading smacks on the beach at Port Gaverne.

Coasting schooners, ketches and trading smacks took the beach at these porths to discharge coal, salt, manure and general supplies. Exports, depending upon the location, included fish, stone, slate, minerals and agricultural produce. Beach trading developed before many of the later harbours were built. At Pentewan, West Polmear and Par, for instance, ships were calling at the beaches to take out minerals before the 18th and 19th century clay ports of St Austell Bay were constructed.

This sometimes risky trade, which called for an intimate knowledge of the coast's weather and sea conditions, continued well into the 20th century. Wherever a cargo awaited collection at an isolated cove, it rendered the delivery of coal or lime profitable for small trading vessels. The beach trade only survived because it helped to extend the useful life of ageing ketches and smacks, although their insurance clubs set strict conditions, usually restricting their calls from April to September. The trading vessels needed to be strongly built. A constant watch was kept on the weather as carts were brought to the water's edge. Motor lorries inevitably won the majority of this trade—delivering small loads to larger ports or to national road carriers. The beach trade faded out between the world wars, and the small trading vessels disappeared from the Cornish coast.

A Cornish beach windlass. Illustration by Charles Napier Hemy.

ASSOCIATED TRADES

Preparing boxes and barrels for fish packing at St. Ives.

Mention has already been made of boatbuilding, but the considerable scale of maritime activity resulted in many trades and businesses on land to support the ships that sailed from Cornwall's ports and harbours. Although rather outside the scope of this book, it must be stressed that, just as with industries today, it was not simply those directly engaged–as members of the crew–who depended on the prosperity of fishing and sea-borne trade.

Very large numbers were employed in St Ives, Newlyn and the other pilchard fisheries gutting, salting and packing the fish. The oil of the pilchard was used for lighting in oil lamps. This resulted in an all-pervading smell which early tourists were recommended to avoid. Murray's *Handbook for Travellers* in 1851 suggested that St Ives 'though highly picturesque, (is) most abominably tainted with the effluvia of the fish cellars'. The huge nets, large enough to surround a shoal, had to be made and maintained, and tanned to preserve the natural fibres of which they were made. The export of pilchards to the mediterranean called for vast supplies of casks,and so every fishing village needed coopers to make these and timber staves were imported to make them,while the village blacksmith would make the iron bands to seal them tightly together.

The fishing boats and larger wooden ships had to be carefully looked after if they were to remain seaworthy. In the days before fibreglass, nylon and polypropylene, timber ships were preserved with natural tar, pitch and bitumen, their joints caulked with oakum and pitch which required regular attention. Their rigging of hemp rope required regular treatment and sails of flax canvas were waxed or tanned. All this gave jobs to men on shore in the boat repair yards, or employment to the fishermen when the season or the weather stopped them going to sea. Despite instances of long working lives for some ships, many did not survive but came to grief on the rocky Cornish coast, or were simply overcome by storms out at sea. It was always a hard and dangerous occupation, especially in the days of sail. The annals of the numerous lifeboat stations record acts of amazing bravery. Members of the maritime community would go off in any weather to man the lifeboats, many hundreds of lives being saved over the years

A glance in *Kelly's Directory of Cornwall*–the Victorian equivalent of our 'Yellow Pages' gives some idea of this landbound side of maritime life. As late as 1897 entries included: 20 Sailmakers, 14 Shipbuilders, 24 Ships' Chandlers, 68 Pilots, 20 Rope and Twine makers and 1 Ships' pump maker. At the same time no less than 261 Master Mariners were listed.

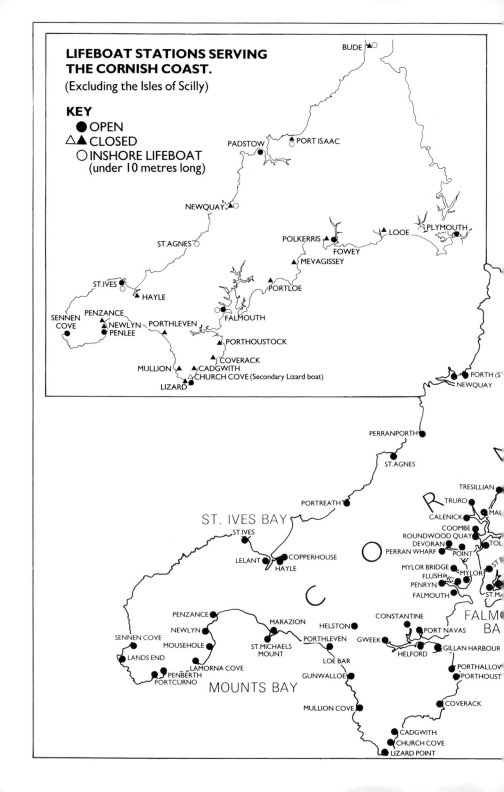

LIFEBOAT STATIONS SERVING THE CORNISH COAST.
(Excluding the Isles of Scilly)

KEY
● OPEN
△▲ CLOSED
○ INSHORE LIFEBOAT
(under 10 metres long)

BUDE

PORT ISAAC
PADSTOW

NEWQUAY

PLYMOUTH
LOOE
POLKERRIS
ST.AGNES
FOWEY
MEVAGISSEY

ST.IVES
PORTLOE
HAYLE

SENNEN COVE
PENZANCE
NEWLYN
PENLEE
PORTHLEVEN
FALMOUTH

PORTHOUSTOCK
COVERACK
MULLION
CADGWITH
CHURCH COVE (Secondary Lizard boat)
LIZARD
PORTH (S?
NEWQUAY

PERRANPORTH

ST.AGNES

TRESILLIAN
TRURO
PORTREATH
CALENICK
MAL
COOMBE
ST. IVES BAY
ROUNDWOOD QUAY
ST.IVES
DEVORAN
TOL
PERRAN WHARF
POINT
LELANT
COPPERHOUSE
HAYLE
MYLOR BRIDGE
MYLOR
FLUSHING
PENRYN
FALMOUTH
ST.M

PENZANCE
CONSTANTINE
FALM
NEWLYN
MARAZION
HELSTON
PORT NAVAS
BA
SENNEN COVE
MOUSEHOLE
PORTHLEVEN
GWEEK
ST.MICHAELS MOUNT
GILLAN HARBOUR
LANDS END
HELFORD
LOE BAR
LAMORNA COVE
PORTHALLOW
PENBERTH
GUNWALLOE
PORTHOUST
PORTCURNO
MOUNTS BAY

COVERACK
MULLION COVE

CADGWITH
CHURCH COVE
LIZARD POINT

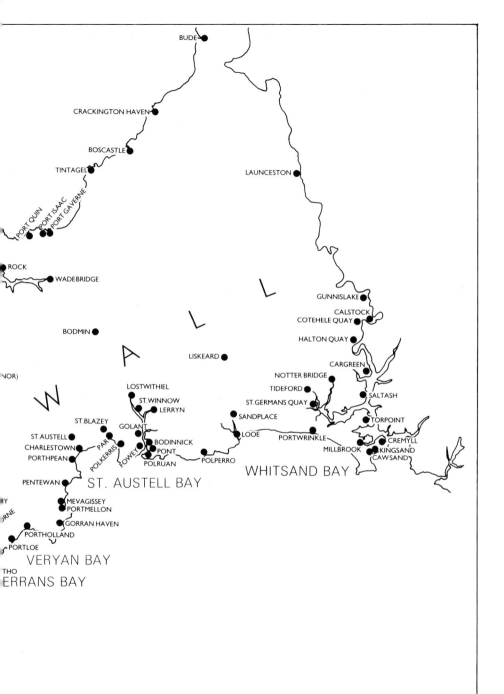

GAZETTEER

With the exception of some twenty miles between Gunnislake on the River Tamar and the site of the Bude Canal terminus, near Launceston, there is hardly a stretch of Cornwall's 300 mile coastline or 100 miles of navigable river estuaries, that cannot claim some association with the county's maritime history.

The following gazetteer is a personal selection of Cornwall's ports and harbours, many of its coastal porths and a selection of its river quays. Most locations are accessible to the public, but a few—especially on river estuaries and harbour waterfrontage—are on private land and permission should be sought from the landowner for access. All of the coastal sites have road access, an important aspect of their development in the first place. However, many of these picturesque coves are rendered less attractive by the intrusion of motor cars, please use the car parks which are invariably provided.

The opportunity should be taken to view the river estuaries of the Tamar, Fowey. Fal and Camel Rivers aboard one of the many excursion boats that operate during the summer season.

The Gazetteer is arranged geographically, starting at the head of navigation on the River Tamar, proceeding along the south coast to Land's End and then returning along the north coast to the Devon border.

Calstock Quay, upstream of the railway viaduct.

CALSTOCK

Once a busy inland shipowning centre and seaport, until local mines declined in the last half of the 19th century. The arrival of rail communication in 1907 and the advent of motor transport during the 1920s finally won its remaining agricultural trade. Frequented by schooners, ketches and barges, in the home, coastal and local trades–and by steam coasters taking out granite from Pearson's quarry in Gunnislake.

The most prominent feature is the railway viaduct, built of concrete blocks. A steam powered wagon hoist, located on the western side of the viaduct at the Calstock end, lowered granite wagons to the quayside; the hoist was removed in the 1930s.Sections of Calstock's old quay walls remain, as do some older quayside buildings. Parts of the house immediately upstream of the viaduct once served as the office of the Devon & Cornwall Steam Packet Co.Ltd., which operated paddle steamers on the River Tamar, including the 110ft. *Empress*, which served as a market boat between Calstock and Devonport until 1925.

SOUTH EAST CORNWALL

TAMAR MANURE NAVIGATION

Completed in 1800, the Tamar Manure Navigation, a canal measuring only 600ft in length, bypassed the fish weir at Weir Head, Gunnislake. Although part of a much grander scheme, vaguely proposing to link with Launceston and Bude, the navigation remained in isolation, but enjoyed a successful and surprisingly long life. Serving the Gunnislake district, a gasworks and brickworks, regular traffic included: manure (lime, sand, 'dock dung' and seaweed), coal, bricks and granite. The canal fell out of use after the first world war. The whole canal is a Scheduled Ancient Monument.

The Tamar market boat Empress. For almost half a century (1880 — 1927) she linked the market garden community in the Tamar Valley to Devonport on market days.

Although generally refered to as Calstock, on the opposite bank of the River–and therefore in Devon–can be seen the site of James Goss' boatyard. On the flat land in front of Ferry Farm, formerly the Ferryboat Inn, many fine small ketch rigged barges were built, culminating in the *Garlandstone*, completed in 1907, and now to be seen at Morwellham where she is to be restored. A fine model of the Goss yard can be seen in the museum at Cotehele Quay.

COTEHELE QUAY

Owned by the National Trust, Cotehele Quay once served the Mount Edgcumbe family's Cotehele House and estate. The quays, limekilns and buildings are carefully maintained. A small maritime museum, depicting the shipping and trade of the River Tamar, has been established by the National Maritime Museum on the ground floor of a quayside warehouse. Also maintained and moored at the quay is the Tamar sailing barge *Shamrock*, which was built by Frederick Hawke of Stone-

house in 1899. She worked the river until 1919 and then spent 42 years in the stone trade, first based on the Lynher river and then working to Porthoustock on the Lizard. Similar vessels working to quays like Cotehele carried supplies of the notorious 'dock dung' or 'night soil' from Devonport's Pottery Quay, for manuring the Tamar Valley's market gardens.

Quay office at Halton.

HALTON QUAY

Halton Quay was the distribution point for market garden produce of the St Dominic area. It was leased to the Plymouth & South Devon Co-operative Society and served by their own fleet of river barges. Lime kilns and the attractive quay office remain, the latter now a small chapel. The grass embankment on the foreshore is not the original quayside, but the quay remains and can still be viewed at low tide, almost covered in riverbank mud.

CARGREEN

The main street of the village ends abruptly at the waters edge. Coastal trading vessels and local barges called at the two sided quay, designed to offer shelter against the action of the tide and river flow. It is difficult to imagine that this quiet village once warranted a revenue cutter to control its smuggling activities.

THE RIVER TAMAR QUAYS ON THE CORNISH BANK

▶ CORNISH QUAYS
▷ DEVON QUAYS

CORNWALL

DEVON

PLYMOUTH

WHITSAND BAY

CAWSAND BAY

1. NEW BRIDGE (GUNNISLAKE)
2. WEIR HEAD
3. CALSTOCK
4. COTEHELE QUAY
5. GREENBANK
6. HALTON QUAY
7. PENTILLE QUAY
8. CLIFTON QUAY
9. CARGREEN
10. PARSONS QUAY
11. LANDULPH QUAY
12. COLLOGGETT QUAY
13. MONDITONHAM QUAY
14. PINEAPPLE QUAY
15. SALTASH
16. WEARDE QUAY
17. FORDER QUAY
18. ANTONY PASSAGE
19. ERTH QUAY
20. TRELUGGAN QUAY
21. POLDRISSICK QUAY
22. NOTTER BRIDGE
23. TIDEFORD
  (KILNA & MORVA QUAYS)
24. ST.GERMANS QUAY
25. POLBATHIC
26. WACKER QUAY
27. TORPONT
28. SOUTHDOWN
29. MILLBROOK (3 QUAYS)
30. ANDERTON
31. CREMYLL QUAY

KINGSMILL LAKE

A beautiful and tranquil creek immediately up stream from Saltash. A series of picturesque quays, Landulph, Pineapple, Moditonham and Colloggett, served the market garden community in the Botus Fleming district. The tiny Moditonham Quay survives intact, with public access, and represents a typical example of the Tamar Valley's agricultural quays, which were once the lifeblood of Tamar barges like *Shamrock*.

SALTASH

A port since the 12th century exporting tin from Dartmoor, Saltash was eclipsed in the 13th century by Plymouth. However, it held jurisdiction over the entire Tamar estuary until this largely symbolic 'authority' was abolished in 1835. Little remains of the town's maritime heritage today, other than its proximity to the waters edge. The maritime quarter of Saltash, known as Waterside, and virtually all of the older waterside features have sadly been demolished. The slipway landing of the Saltash Chain Ferry, which was replaced by the suspension bridge in 1961, is still evident, as are parts of the Passage House Inn–rather pointlessly renamed The Boatman Inn in 1981. A part of the Town Quay is still in use, but a pontoon landing used to extend from the end, providing facilities for the paddle steamers of the Saltash Three Towns & District Steamboat Co Ltd, once the largest river steamer fleet in the South West.

THE RIVERS LYNHER & TIDDY

Quays and landings on the combined estuary of the two rivers included Antony Passage, from where a passenger ferry crossed to Jupiter Point on the Antony shore and Jessops' Quarry quay in Forder Creek, which was served by Jessops' own river barges. Wacker Quay, on the southern shore, was used by the War Department to land supplies and ordnance for Scraesdon and Tregantle Forts and remains of the military railway can still be detected at the quay.

Treluggan and Poldrissick Quays on the River Lynher were busy in the 'blue elvan' roadstone trade until the 1950s, frequented by Tamar barges, ketches, schooners and later by Dutch motor coasters. The hulks of the schooner *Millom Castle*–one of the last trading vessels to discharge at Cargreen–and, rather appropriately, the river barge *Lynher*, are to be seen quietly rotting away at Poldrissick. Permission must be sought from the landowner to visit the quay.

Beyond the mouth of the Lynher, the River Tiddy continues to St Germans Quay. This entire stretch of estuary, from its mouth at the Hamoaze to St Germans Quay is known as the St Germans River. Once an important trading place for the St Germans district, the large quay, warehouse and quayside cottages all remain in a beautiful setting beneath the St Germans railway viaduct. The Tiddy was navigable for small barges right up to Tideford.

One of the Thornycroft of Southampton built floating bridges of 1960 pictured at Torpoint with the Ferrybus in 1982. The ferry is the only floating, bus fare-stage in the country.

TORPOINT

Developed during the late 18th century by the Carew family of Antony, Torpoint served as a graving beach for naval and other ships. Here ships were careened for maintenance, re-caulking and tarring (at Tar Point). A substantially built ballast pond from this period is a prominent feature offshore. Merchant ships sailing light and Naval vessels without full provisions or ordnance required ballast–stone, scrap etc–to maintain their required sailing draught. A turnpike road from Torpoint was built to link with the older Saltash to Cremyll road. In 1791 the newly established Torpoint Ferry won the Royal Mail contract for the Cornish mail from the Cremyll Ferry. In 1834 the first chain ferry was introduced, designed by James Rendel. The Torpoint Ferry remains as an important Tamar crossing with considerable commuter traffic to Plymouth. The three ferries now in use were built during the 1960s and all three were lengthened during 1987/8; they now carry the names *Tamar*, *Lynher* and, rather inappropriately, *Plym*.

Both the outlook and a distinctly naval atmosphere along the Torpoint foreshore bear witness to the town's close association with the Royal Dockyard at Devonport, on the opposite shore. HMS Fisgard, the Royal Navy training base, is located on the outskirts of Torpoint. The firing ranges of the base occupy a part of the shoreline along the adjacent St Johns Lake.

MILLBROOK LAKE

Quays at Southdown date from 1650, when a gunpowder works was establised and the 1730s, when the King's Brewhouse was built. Beer rather than water was supplied on Naval ships at the time, due to its superior keeping qualities and 20,000 gallons a week could be brewed here to supply the Devonport-based fleet. At Foss, local passenger boats are repaired alongside the tide mill building which was once owned by miller John Parsons, who founded the Millbrook Steamboat Company in 1900. The playing field now located behind the mill building was the mill pond. At Millbrook, storehouses and limekilns, once sited at the waters edge, are now stranded inland as a result of infilling schemes. At the end of Moles-worth Terrace there stood two piers, each used by opposing Millbrook and Saltash based steamboat companies which competed vigorously for the lucrative passenger trade between Millbrook Lake and Devonport.

At Anderton, on a small point of land, are the remains of a boatbuilding yard where James and John Waterman once built wooden vessels. In the 1880s they moved their business to Cremyll.

Note: Most creeks within the Port of Plymouth are known as 'lakes'.

The Cremyll Ferry boat Northern Belle in 1985.

CREMYLL

Since the 1930s Mashfords have occupied the boatyards and slipways where the Waterman brothers and Rogers & Co built small wooden vessels and steamboats. The Cremyll Ferry runs from here to Admiral's Hard in Stonehouse. This ancient ferry belonged to the Mt.Edgcumbe Estate until it was taken over by the Millbrook Steamboat Company in 1946. The *Northern Belle*, which currently maintains the service, has been doing so for over 60 years. She was originally built as the steamboat *Armadillo* in 1926, by Rogers & Co. ·

Cremyll Quay, which was developed by James Rendel in 1836-37, additionaly served as a landing for vessels trading with the Mt.Edgcumbe Estate.

Millbrook Lake with Foss Brickworks on the left and Southdown on the right. In the background Torpoint is on the left, Devoport on the right, divided by the River Tamar.

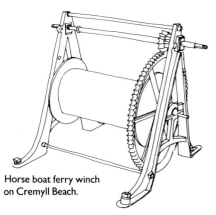

Horse boat ferry winch on Cremyll Beach.

KINGSAND & CAWSAND

Until 1840 Kingsand lay within the county of Devon, the stream behind the Halfway House Inn and a mark on the wall of a house in Garret Street serve to indicate the old boundary. The villages of Kingsand and Cawsand supported a fleet of small fishing smacks, or 'hookers', and pilchard seines. Since Elizabethan times, fish were landed at nearby Pier Cellars, which, since 1889, has remained in government ownership but has now been totally redeveloped. The wall of the fish cellars in Cawsand remains, but has been incorporated into a holiday development.

Some pilot boats for the Port of Plymouth were also based here. Cawsand Bay has long offered a sheltered anchorage from all except south easterly gales. In this century the bay has offered anchorage to transatlantic and other liners, calling in at Plymouth to disembark passengers and mail.

Villagers were also active in the free trade. Smuggled goods landed at or near the villages, out of sight from officials in Plymouth, later made their way across the Tamar. Overlooking the beaches from Penlee Woods are the Old Coastguard Cottages, built in the 1820s to curb smuggling in the bay.

Cawsand with watermen's passenger boats from Plymouth on the beach.

PORTWRINKLE

A fishing village in Whitsand Bay largely redeveloped. The fish cellars survive, but are in a poor state of repair. A small refuge harbour also survives.

LOOE

An ancient port at the confluence of the East and West Looe rivers, Looe was a seaport for the Caradon mining district. East Looe and West Looe were at one time separate boroughs. A fishing fleet is still maintained on the quay in East Looe and a new fish market indicates a recent revival in its prosperity The Banjo Pier extends from East Looe, forming a breakwater and offering protection against easterly and south easterly gales.

Quays now serving as car parks were once busy mineral quays, exporting copper ore and granite and importing coal for mine engines. The car park upstream of the bridge occupies the site of a goods yard for the Liskeard and Looe Railway which replaced the earlier six mile long Liskeard & Looe Union Canal, opened in 1828. The lock gates of the canal, long since derelict, can still be detected at Terras, near the head of the tidal estuary of the East Looe River. The limekilns still survive along the line of the canal and a canal basin at Sandplace was still navigable long after the remaining stretch of the canal was closed.

Looe.

POLPERRO

Polperro supported seining and drift fishing. Its inner drying tidal harbour is protected by double piers with a narrow entrance, which could be protected by lowering timber baulks into slots at the end of each pier. Smuggling was a staple trade. Lord of the manor in which Polperro was situated, was Zephaniah Job, a banker and merchant. So scrupulously honest was he considered by the local population that he was employed by the smugglers to look after their affairs!

The type of small gaff rigged fishing vessels pictured here at Polperro were developed in the harbour.

FOWEY & ST. AUSTELL BAY

POLRUAN

The village of Polruan lies just inside the mouth of the River Fowey. There is a mid 19th century coastguard watch house near the car park, at the top of the village. A passenger ferry operates all year round, crossing the harbour from the end of Fore Street in Polruan to Whitehouse Slip, Fowey. Polruan was a busy boat and ship building village; much evidence of past ventures survive. William Geach & Son built sloops and smacks until c1840, near the entrance of the harbour. The Slade family occupied a yard off West Street from 1856 until 1929. The hopper barge *Lantic Bay*, usually moored off Polruan, was built by the Brazen Island Shipyard of Polruan. Most of the Polruan waterfront upstream of Ferry Quay is still engaged in boatbuilding and yacht repair. The ship repair facilities of the Fowey Harbour Commissioners are located upstream, at the far end of the village.

PONT PILL

The quay at Pont, once frequented by ketches and barges, is owned by the National Trust and its limekiln, quay office and warehouse are carefully

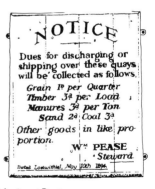

Quayside sign at Pont.

preserved, providing a good example of a Cornish agricultural community's river quay.

BODINNICK

The steep main street through the village descends to the slipway of the ancient Bodinnick Ferry. The ferry today is maintained by two vehicle pontoons, manoeuvred by motor launches. The house and garden immediately downstream of the ferry slip was once a ship building yard, owned variously by Nicholas Butson, John Marks and William Rendle.

LERRYN & ST.WINNOW

Navigable up to the road bridge in Lerryn Village, the River Lerryn supported the maritime trade of the local agricultural community. Evidence of this maritime activity survives in the shape of lime kilns and waterside warehouses in the village. There is a beautiful quayside location, once a farm hard, just upstream from Lerryn, on the River Fowey itself, on the shore below the churchyard of St Winnow.

The River Fowey at St. Winnow.

LOSTWITHIEL

Evidence survives of Lostwithiel's agricultural trade in a bank of limekilns and riverside buildings, which owe their existence to past river trade. The town's quays now seem hopelessly un-navigable, but Lostwithiel can still be reached in a small boat, on a spring tide.

Established as a port for Bodmin, Lostwithiel was one of the County's foremost trading ports from the 12th to the mid 14th century, after which silt from tin streaming works began to choke the river, although some barge traffic continued right up to the beginning of this century. Lostwithiel continued to collect keelage and anchorage dues from ships in the river until the Fowey Harbour Board was established in 1870. Lostwithiel's privilege of holding a maritime court is still symbolised by the town's use of a miniature silver oar as one of its maces.

RIVER FOWEY CLAY WHARVES

A series of river quays occupy the western bank of the River Fowey, opposite St Winnow, at Golant and below Colvithick Wood. These riverside quays have largely been isolated from the farming communities they once served, by the railway which runs along the shoreline from Lostwithiel to the extensive clay wharves and loading jetties opposite Mixtow and Bodinnick. The clay wharves of Fowey and the harbour of Par are linked by a private road–the former trackbed of the Cornwall Minerals Railway.

Clay, brought down by train, is loaded directly into the holds of ships in a highly mechanised and efficient way using the latest technology. These busy clay wharves are mostly hidden from view from Fowey itself, but it is an impressive sight to see ships, some over 10,000 tons, slowly pass by only yards away from the Town Quay . The best viewpoints are gained from the shore line around Mixtow or, even better, by boat. A number of launches or small motor boats are available for hire from the Town Quay in Fowey.

River Fowey ferryboat 'Tamsin'.

FOWEY

The waterfront of Fowey town owes its haphazard and picturesque appearance to centuries of building and re-building. An ancient fishing hamlet, then medieval port, Fowey also became a centre for piracy. Mark Mixtow was one of the town's most notorious privateers. Licenced by the Crown to attack French ships, *he* extended this authority to include most shipping in the English Channel! In the 16th century Fowey settled to general trading. The greatest change to the port's fortunes came late in the 19th century, with the construction of the clay wharves up-river.

As in most riverside cities and towns today, public access to the waterfront has become limited. The main public quays and slipways are to be found at Readymoney Cove, at the harbour mouth and Whitehouse Slip, the landing place for the Polruan Ferry and notable for the distinctive harbour light, a red-painted iron structure of 1892, which dominates the view from the lane leading to the slip. Town Quay is very much the waterside centre of Fowey while at Albert Quay a pontoon landing now serves the swollen, summer season, maritime community. To the north, Caffa Mill Pill, once the site of the Heller family's shipyard, is now filled in as a car park and for access to the Bodinnick vehicle ferry. The ferry has only recently been

Fowey Harbour lead in light at Whitehouse Slip.

moved from its old, steep and inconvenient slipway which can be seen beside the Riverside Hotel. Boat building yards, sail lofts and chandlers occupied the waterfront. Some still do, but many of these premises are converted to serve the holiday industry. The Hall Walk along the opposite tree lined bank of the harbour provides spectacular views of Fowey, Polruan and the coast to Dodman Point. Closer inspection of Fowey's waterfront can only be gained from the water itself.

POLKERRIS

A picturesque sandy cove in St Austell Bay. Polkerris once engaged in pilchard fishing and the remains of the fish cellar can still be seen, claimed to be the largest in Cornwall. Its protecting pier was built in 1735. From 1859 to 1922 a lifeboat was stationed here, and the old lifeboat house still stands, opposite the inn.

PAR

The tide once reached St Blazey, where a bridge crossed the Luxulyan River and a ferry crossed the estuary at Par at high tide. Silt, generated by tin streaming, choked the narrow estuary and by the end of the 19th century the sea had receded. Ships beached on the extensive sandbanks near Par to load minerals. Granite for both Rudyeard's and Smeaton's Eddystone Lighthouses were loaded in this way.

Developed by J.T.Treffry to serve his mines and quarries, Par Harbour was reclaimed from the sand banks and completed in 1840. Intense industrial activity within the docks and around its immediate vicinity may still be witnessed, in terms of both extensive industrial remains and the continuing importance of the harbour in the clay trade. Original installations included a lead smelting works, brickworks, pilchard fishery, shipbuilding yard, granite dressing yard and a candle factory—for the mining industry.

Par became a shipbuilding and shipowning community, building schooners for the Newfoundland and Home trades. Benjamin Tregaskes maintained one of the last wooden ship repair yards in the country, catering for the rapidly declining fleet of coastal ketches and schooners. In the last century though, some 10 schooners and barquentines were built up to 250 tons. The dry dock, the only one between Falmouth and Plymouth continued in use until 1957. The renowned ship portrait painter Rueben Chappel was also based at Par, painting steam coasters and Britain's last sail trading vessels.

CHARLESTOWN

Charlestown was developed by Charles Rashleigh, a local landowner and mining adventurer. In 1791 he began excavations in the cove of West Polmear, where trading vessels took the beach to discharge and load cargoes. The works were completed in 1801, to the plan of John Smeaton, specially designed to transport copper ore from nearby mines; soon china clay was to become the dominant trade of the port, and has resulted in its survival to this day as a working harbour. The present cobbled car park areas were storage areas for copper and china clay; much else remains of this late 18th century harbour village including a delightful hexagonal harbour office overlooking the outer basin. In addition there was a shipyard, ropewalk, pilchard fishery, warehouses, limekiln, brickworks—indeed everything needed in a self-sufficient maritime community.

Dry clay from the storage linhays, like the large building behind the 'Shipwreck Centre' was carried by a tramway beneath the quay road to the loading shutes. Similar shutes in evidence today are designed to work from road level. The lower quay, on the west, was used chiefly for unloading coal and cask staves from the Baltic at a time when much china clay was exported in barrels.

Amongst the more 'popular' exhibits in the Shipwreck Centre are to be found useful details of the village's interesting maritime history.

The harbour office at Charlestown.

Pentewan Harbour 1988

PENTEWAN

Another clay and minerals harbour, developed in the 19th century, Pentewan was built by the local landowner, Sir Charles Hawkins. It was opened in 1826 and within three years a tramway was built to link the harbour with St Austell. The narrow gauge line was converted to steam traction in 1872.

Plagued throughout its life with silting problems in the harbour mouth, Pentewan effectively lost its clay traffic after 1919. The last trading vessels called for sand and concrete cargoes in the 1940s.

However, the dock remains intact, with water in the basin. The lock gates and winches are still in situ as are many dockside buildings, including the Harbourmaster's house, weighbridge and stores. Beyond the lock gates, towards the sea, Pentewan's silting problem is plainly evident. The channel, jetty and breakwater are virtually buried beneath sand, which has built up for many years. Rails laid along the outer jetty owe their existence to a concrete block and sand works which was established before the first World War.

MEVAGISSEY

In contrast to the more recent clay ports of St Austell Bay, Mevagissey's history dates back centuries to medieval times and owes its existence, not to the wealth of the land but, to fishing, in particular pilchard seining.

In the early 19th century there were 30 pilchard seines registered in the harbour and by 1850 Mevagissey supported some 80 fishing vessels. Fishing continues today, although pleasure boats of various types are numerous also.

The first stone built, protecting pier was built during the 15th century. In 1775 an Act was obtained to build a pier enclosing the present day inner harbour. Exposed to south easterly gales, the pier suffered continual damage. During the 1880s the two piers forming the outer harbour were built.

There was a lifeboat station at Mevagissey from 1869 until 1930.

PORTMELLON

One of the important 20th century boatbuilding yards is situated here. Percy Mitchell built many fine working boats and yachts of various kinds, up to about 50ft length, which then had to be hauled along the road for launching.

GORRAN HAVEN

A sandy cove protected by a jetty, Gorran Haven supported both seine and drift boats, while general trade usually involved transshipment of goods for Gorran at Fowey onto small lighters. Its 15th century pier was rebuilt in 1820 and reconstructed in 1888.

FALMOUTH BAY

PORTLOE

A particularly attractive fishing village set amid spectacular cliff scenery. Portloe once supported a small drift fleet and a seine fishery. The natural harbour has no jetties, so trading ketches took the beach. Notable near the harbour mouth is the extremely steep lifeboat slipway. The lifeboat house survives, converted for domestic use. Sufficient fishing and lobster potting continues to provide Portloe with an authentic air.

PORTSCATHO

A pilchard seining village in Gerrans Bay, noted for the smuggling activities of its villagers.

Portscatho.

ST.MAWES

St.Mawes is a beautifully located fishing village which once maintained pilchard, crabbing and oyster fisheries. St Mawes' first stone pier was built in 1536 and the St Mawes Pier & Harbour Company improved the pier and harbour in 1854. St Mawes Castle was built as part of the coastal defences of

Henry VIII, with Pendennis Castle at Falmouth, to protect the Carrick Roads.

Some Falmouth Harbour pilots were also based here, the location proving more suitable than Falmouth, both for seeing incoming ships and getting out to sea aboard their pilot cutters. The Peters family's small boatyard, begun in 1790, was famous for the fast six-oared pilot gigs; the racing of these gigs, which takes place in the summer, has become popular and now more gigs are being built to the same•pattern that Peters was using in the early 1800s.

Because of its sheltered location overlooking the Roads, St Mawes has evolved into a holiday and retirement resort. The process of change began during the late 19th century following the arrival of the railway in Falmouth and the establishment of a passenger steamer service. St Mawes today forms a good mooring for yachts, but little remains of the original fishing village or the local atmosphere.

PERCUIL RIVER QUAYS

Opposite St Mawes lies Place House, now a hotel. There is a slipway adjacent to the house which served the house and estate and provided a landing for the twice daily mail steamer from Falmouth. On Cellars Beach, near Amsterdam Point, a boatyard once built pilot cutters, fishing boats, quay punts and other small boats. Trewince Quay served Trewince Farm in Porth Creek.

Trewince Farm Quay in Porth Creek on the Percuil River.

Percuil was a river trading quay of some importance owing in part to its ferry across the river between the St Mawes and Gerrans districts. Ketches and barges discharged on the shore. A wagonette ran twice daily from Gerrans to meet the St Mawes steamer with passengers and mail. The shore was also used to careen ships *i.e.* beaching them to lean on one side of their keel for the purpose of cleaning, re-caulking and repair. Little,

except the stone ferry steps on either side of the river, remains of the hamlet. The site is now used by small boat owners.

Polingey Quay and Trethem Quay each served farms of the same name, in creeks of the same name. These two beautiful creeks are best observed from the National Trust land on the road down to Percuil.

ST.JUST

St.Just's convenient location in the Carrick Roadstead has so far escaped development as a port. But it has not escaped notice over the years. Schemes promoted for St Just Pool over the years have included a Royal Naval Dockyard (18th century), a railway terminus from the china clay district (19th century), a transatlantic liner port (early 20th century) and more recently, a container port! In the event St Just Pool has been host to the training ship HMS Ganges, provided quarantine anchorage for the port of Falmouth and supported a boatyard and a small fishing community.

KING HARRY & TOLVERNE REACHES OF THE RIVER FAL

Turnaware Point, King Harry Ferry and Tolverne Cottage each provide excellent viewpoints for these stretches of the river. The King Harry Ferry is an ancient crossing. The first chain ferry was introduced in 1889. There have been six ferries or 'chain bridges'–three steam and three diesel. The current ferry was built in 1974 by Dredge Marine of Ponsharden.

At times this crossing provides spectacular views of ocean going shipping laid up in the King Harry and Tolverne reaches. A visit to Tolverne Smugglers' Cottage restaurant will offer excellent views of Tolverne Reach, while inside the cottage is a virtual museum of memorabilia from ships that have been laid up in the Fal.

A River Fal excursion boat passes laid-up shipping in the Fal in 1984.

Truro in the 1950's. The warehouse and building on the right was owned by Coast Lines Ltd.

RUAN LANIHORNE

The hamlet gives its name to the creek–the Ruan River–upon which stand two quays. One quay, in the village, is now silted up, but the second, near the mouth of the creek, is still navigable to small boats.

TREGONY

A medieval port until the tide began receding during the 15th century. Some evidence suggests that the River Fal might have been navigable further upstream to a place near the present day Golden Mill. Until 1740, when the Sett Bridge was built over the Fal near Ruan Lanihorne, the river was navigable to Penvose Quay, which served Penvose Farm.

THE TRESILLIAN RIVER

The village of Malpas faces Malpas Passage across the mouth of the Tresillian River. An ancient ferry crossed here until recently. A horse boat was also available for the passage of carriages and carts. Below Malpas Road, at the point where the Truro river converges, there stood the shipyard of William Scoble and John Davies, who built schooners, ketches, barges and steamers.

Barges plied to Tresillian Quay at the head of navigation, carrying general cargoes and barley for the maltings. The County Council's depot was established here with a quay for deliveries of roadstone brought up the river by barge from quarries at Porthoustock on the Lizard.

TRURO

Quays have existed at the confluence of the Rivers Kenwyn and Allen for over eight centuries. During the 14th century tin was smelted in works near the river's edge and shipped out from Truro's quays. Once the authority for almost the entire Fal Estuary, the port now extends only to the St Just and Mylor Pools in the Carrick Roadstead.

Only a small stretch of Lemon Quay–one of the earliest trading quays–survives. The majority of the quay and the River Kenwyn along which it stood, is covered over to form a car park. At the point of land formed by the confluence of Truro's two rivers is Town Quay. The large concrete building on the quay was built for Coast Lines Ltd and replaced an earlier warehouse . The Harbourmaster's office alongside dates back to the last century. Opposite Town Quay, adjoining the ring road, is Worth's Quay, a landing place for passenger boats from Falmouth since at least the 1870's.

From the Radio Cornwall building, backing onto Malpas Road are a range of warehouses which were, until recently, named Trafalgar Wharf. Immediately downstream of Town Quay is Garras Wharf, once the warehouses and timber ponds of Harveys timber merchants, but now totally redeveloped.

The limited navigation available on the Truro River can be observed from Boscawen Park at low tide. The winding river channel is plainly discernable in the muddy estuary.

Below Boscawen Park is Sunny Corner, where Charles Dyer built wooden trading vessels on the banks of the river.

COOMBE CREEK

Roundwood Quay stands at the confluence of Coombe and Lamouth Creeks. This large river quay was once owned by R.A.Daniell, a wealthy local land owner and mining adventurer. Minerals were shipped from here until the wharves at Devoran were developed in the early 19th century. The quay saw further use as an additional building slip for Henry Stephens Trethowan, a shipbuilder of Little Falmouth. Publicised as the Plum Gardens, Roundwood was also frequented by excursion steamers from Falmouth. The steamers of Benney & Co of Truro and the River Fal Steamship Company, landed passengers to enjoy the local Kea plums.

The riverside community of Coombe engaged in oyster dredging and shrimping. The 'Coombe Creekers' also maintained a fleet of lighters to attend ships with too deep a draught to reach Truro, which had moored at Woodbury.

An alternative name for Coombe Creek was Cowlands Creek, as Cowlands Farm and quay lay at the head of navigation. Local nomenclature such as this has survived along many stretches of navigable Cornish estuaries. In the days when the waterways were the main highways for local traffic–barges, steamers etc–these names were applied in much the same way as we talk of the 'Truro Road' or the 'Coombe Road'.

PILL CREEK

Once the site of mineral quays and a shipbuilding yard. A large quay remains on the western bank.

RESTRONGUET CREEK

Yard Point, just inside the mouth of the creek, was the location for the shipyard of John Stephens. He and his shipwright, Peter Ferris, built schooners and ketches.

Point, in Penpoll Creek, was an industrialised area, with busy wharves and a tin smelting works.

The tug Perran towing a brigantine in Restronguet Creek.

Devoran was developed by the Redruth & Chasewater Railway Company in 1824, to serve their 4ft gauge mineral railway. The wharves at Devoran grew into a substantial riverside port, but were plagued by silting problems throughout their history. The wharves fell into disuse once the railway closed in 1915. Their remains can still be seen in this, now silent backwater, with extensive stone-built ore storage bins and massive granite bollards along the line of the quay.

At Perran Wharf Welsh coal and Scandinavian timber (after which the nearby Norway Inn was named) was imported, for the nearby mining districts. In 1791 the Perran Foundry was established by the Fox family of Falmouth. The Foundry buildings were converted to a mill in 1897 and survive today. A Perran Foundry Trust is being established and it is hoped to restore the buildings.

MYLOR CREEK

A Naval Dockyard was established in Mylor Pool during the 19th century, to supply Naval vessels with water and ordnance and to serve the training ship HMS Ganges. There was a cooperage and an Admiralty burial ground nearby. The substantial quays remain as part of the Mylor Yacht Harbour. In Mylor Churchyard are buried some of Falmouth's Post Office Packet captains as well as Thomas James who on the evening of the 7th of Dec 1814 on his return to Flushing from St-Mawes in a boat, was shot by a Custom House Officer and expired in a few hours after.

Officious zeal in luckless hour laid wait
And wilful sent the mourd'rous ball of fate
JAMES to his home (which late in health he left)
Wounded returns, of life is soon bereft.

In the same churchyard lies a shipwright who died in 1770, the gravestone reads

Alass friend Joseph
his end was all most sudden
As though the mandate came
express from heaven
His foot it slip and he did fall
Help Help he cries and that was all.

FLUSHING

The waterfront which survives today was largely developed during the 17th century by Samuel Trefusis, a local landowner. The dry stone construction of the quay walls have stood the test of time and are said to be the work of Dutch engineers employed by Trefusis.

The Flushing Ferry runs from Old Quay. Since the 17th century at least, this ferry ran to Greenbank

Quay, directly opposite, but following the introduction of steamboats in the 1870s, the opportunity was taken to alter the route to land at Market Strand, nearer the centre of Falmouth. Watermen in their quay punts still offered passage to Greenbank and other stations in Falmouth Harbour. A wooden watermen's shelter survives at the back of the quay. Adjacent to the watermen's shelter is the last remaining wall of Samuel Trefusis' Great Cellars, a warehouse built for the Post Office Packet trade.

Upstream from Flushing is the slipway of Falmouth Boat Construction at Little Falmouth. From this site, many Falmouth Packets were launched and Henry Stephens Trethowan later built trading vessels.

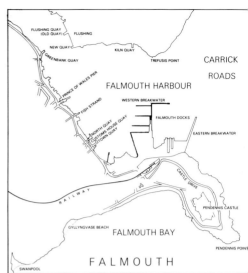

PENRYN

At the head of navigation on the Penryn River, Penryn was a medieval victualling port which once held jurisdiction over the entire stretch of water that is now Falmouth Harbour. While Penryn's importance as a Port Authority ended in 1652, when the Customs House was removed to the developing harbour of Smithwick (later renamed Falmouth), its trade continued well into the 20th century. Evidence of Penryn's extensive warehousing and quayside facilities, remain to be seen, both in derelict buildings and in the continued use of quayside warehouses–albeit now served from road rather than river.

Trade at Penryn included the export of granite from Freemans' numerous quarries nearby, and the unusual import trade of live cattle from Corunna, until public concern regarding the animals' welfare forced its end. Ketches and barges maintained a general trade, serving the nearby agricultural community and landing coal supplies.

FALMOUTH

Falmouth's waterfront has recently been discovered by developers and is currently the subject of many schemes. Each development is 'exclusive', both in terms of the purchasers they will undoubtedly attract and for the sad reduction in public access to the waterfront. In common with many footpaths, public right of way to the water via lanes and steps needs to be maintained. But little or no public outcry has been made about their wholesale loss in recent years.

Greenbank Quay remains at the northern end of the harbour. The beach alongside was used as a graving beach for the annual careening of harbour vessels, like the passenger tug Victor. The waterfront from Greenbank Park to the Royal Cornwall Yacht Club, was once owned by the Olver family who maintained quays and warehouses for their building, contracting and general merchants trades. A number of building slips, quays and warehouses existed along Admiral's Quay up to the Prince of Wales Pier. Their haphazard development was characteristic of any busy 19th century waterfront. These quays suffered decline during this century, probably due more to chronic disrepair than lack of commercial use. Within the past decade most of the buildings have gone, replaced by waterside apartments.

The foundation stone of the Prince of Wales Pier was laid by the Prince of Wales in 1903. Construction was completed in 1905. Post war modernisation has sadly destroyed the original Edwardian shelters and lamp standards. Observation of the stonework at the pier will reveal a number of different stone courses and building styles. The oldest part, near the pier approaches, are believed to date back to the 17th century. A quay on this Market Strand site was completed in 1873 and extended five years later. Virtually the entire Market Strand Quay is still discernable from the difference in the stone work at the landward end of the pier.

Fish Strand Quay served the nearby fish market and landed mail from the Post Office Packets. In 1688 Falmouth packets won the contract for the Corunna mail, followed later by contracts for Lisbon, West Indies, North America, Bermuda, Jamaica and Brazil. In 1827 some forty packets were based at Falmouth. The introduction of steam signalled their decline. By 1850 Southampton had replaced Falmouth as the main port for foreign mails.

The car park adjacent to the Fish Strand Quay was the site of Falmouth's gasworks, coal being discharged directly from colliers at the gasworks own quay.

A series of quays, mostly built upon, back off Arwenack Street and extend all the way to the North, Customs House and Town Quays. These three quays enclose the Inner Basin. Parts of North and Customs House Quays date from the 17th century. On Customs House Quay, running parallel to Arwenack Street, are the Harbourmaster's Office, Customs House (1814) and a brick chimney known as the Queen's Pipe, which was built in the 19th century to burn contraband tobacco. At the entrance to Town Quay stands a whitewashed watermen's shelter. In Arwenack Street, opposite the access road to the basin, are the red brick shipping offices of G C Fox, established here in 1790.

The area of land between the above mentioned quays and Falmouth Docks has been gradually infilled and is currently the subject of a major development scheme. This semi-derelict area, which sweeps around to The Bar, was once occupied by a tide pool and the slipways of steel shipbuilders: W.H.Lean, Charles Burt, Messrs Pool, Skinner & Williams, and Falmouths premier steel ship builder, Cox & Co.

Falmouth Docks. The Falmouth harbour tugs St. Agnes and Lynch attend the oil tanker Esso Yorkshire.

Below the headland of Pendennis lay the modern ship repair docks, founded in 1860. A good viewpoint of the docks and Falmouth Harbour can be obtained from the Castle Drive, directly above the docks. Coin operated telescopes are available.

Falmouth's Maritime Museum in Bell's Court is well worth a visit and many aspects of the harbour and river trade are depicted. The Falmouth steam tug St Dennis is permanently moored and open to visitors on North Quay, as part of the museum.

On many evenings throughout the year, Falmouth's gaff cutter 'Working Boats' race. This class of sailing vessel has evolved from the Quay Punt, a boat which raced out to meet incoming vessels and claim the right to tender for her whilst she was moored in the roadstead. Similar vessels dredged for oysters in the estuary, as the use of motor boats over the oyster beds was prohibited.

HELFORD RIVER QUAYS

The estuary is lined with a number of river quays and other landing places, which served the Helford estuary's agricultural communities.

Vessels trading to the Glendurgan Estate, took the beach at Durgan. Merthen Manor supported its own quay in Polwheveral Creek and its own ketch, the Rob Roy, while Norwegian timber boats reached this point with timber for the mines.

Scotts Quay, downstream from Merthen, exported granite from Constantine, as did Porth Navas Quay, although Porth Navas is more closely associated with oyster farming.

Boat yards still line the final navigable stretch of the estuary to Gweek and Gweek Quay which once served as a port for Helston, growing in importance in medieval times as the Loe Bar formed, restricting navigation of the River Cober to Helston.

Helford once supported a Customs House for the estuary. From here a ferry, of ancient origin, crosses to Helford Passage.

At the mouth of the estuary, on the southern shore, is the attractive Gillan Harbour, a sheltered creek, with a tide mill at its head. Gillan supported its own trading fleet in medieval times.

THE LIZARD

PORTHOUSTOCK

A fishing cove dominated by the loading jetties of the adjacent roadstone quarries. It was to these Lizard quarries that river barges of the Fal estuary came, loading roadstone under the shutes and taking it to Tresillian Quay. The shutes went out of use in 1958. There were similar shutes in use at nearby Dean Quarry.

Porthoustock was a lifeboat station from 1869 to 1945. In the churchyard of St.Keverne, above Porthoustock, is the Mohegan Memorial which commemorates the wreck of that liner on the Manacle Rocks off Porthoustock in 1898, with the loss of 106 lives.

COVERACK

A pilchard fishing and crab potting village, the small harbour is built of the local serpentine stone, with an inscribed stone dated 1724.

CADGWITH

Pilchard seining, crab potting and smuggling have all thrived here. A lifeboat arrived in 1867, but the station was amalgamated with the Lizard station in 1961, with the opening of a new base at Kilcobben Cove.

CHURCH COVE (LANDEWEDNACK)

The pilchard cellars building remains. There is also a boat winch at the top of the extremely steep slipway. The lifeboat house was for the reserve Lizard boat, launched from here if weather conditions were unsuitable in Polpeor Cove. The station closed in 1899 after just two service launches.

POLPEOR COVE (THE LIZARD)

The most southerly point on the British mainland. The cove saw some beach trading, and the Lizard Lifeboat was stationed here from 1859 to 1960.

MOUNT'S BAY & LANDS END

MULLION COVE

A fishing village with a protective pier which supported pilchard seines but as there were no curing cellars in the village, the fish were taken to Newlyn. There was a lifeboat here from 1867 to 1908.

PORTHLEVEN

A fishing village prior to the building of the present harbour. which was completed in 1818. These works, on the exposed south-west facing coast of Mount's Bay were destroyed in a storm in 1824 and subsequently rebuilt. The promoters of the development sought general and mining trade—coal and timber in, minerals out. The harbour did not prove satisfactory and the venture failed; the company was bought out by Harveys of Hayle in 1855. Harveys improved the harbour, building the long breakwater to protect the entrance and trade increased. But despite this phase Porthleven has continued much as it did before, as a fishing and boatbuilding harbour, though with an extensive inner basin, the legacy of Harveys' never fulfilled plans.

PRUSSIA COVE

This small cove has been immortalised through *An autobiography of a Cornish Smuggler*, based on the exploits of the Carter family. John Carter, known as the 'King of Prussia', and his brother, were local smugglers towards the end of the 18th century. When the Revenue men seized a cargo, Carter broke into Penzance Custom House, apparently only recovering his own property, leaving others' alone. At one time, during the Ameri-

can War, when a Revenue cutter came close to the shore, Carter fired on it using a coastal defence battery.

ST MICHAEL'S MOUNT

There is an ancient harbour on the island, which is linked to Marazion by a causeway. The first pier was built during the 15th century. In 1727 the St Aubyn family extended the pier and improved the harbour. In 1821 the pier was extended again. Salt fish, tin and copper ore were transported by pack horse over the causeway for export from the harbour. Imports included coal, iron, timber and corn.

Lord St Levan still resides on the Mount, but it is now owned by the National Trust. Two of the 19th century rowing barges, which were used as ferries, have survived.

On the piers are to be seen old cannon barrels used as bollards, while on the east pier is the footprint of Queen Victoria, in cement, commemorating her visit to the Mount in 1846.

PENZANCE

An early Mounts Bay fishing centre, Penzance was also a Coinage Town and tin exporter during the 17th century. The Old Pier was built in 1766 and extended in 1785 and 1812. The Albert Pier was completed in 1853 Other major harbour works of the 19th century included the construction of a floating harbour in 1884. A private dry dock was built by Nicholas Holman's foundry in 1880, to replace an older one; they still operate the dock. When the new road to the railway station was built along the harbour front, the Ross Swing Bridge was put in to enable vessels to enter the dry dock.

The Trinity House Depot was established at Penzance in 1866. It serviced lighthouses and navigational markers from Trevose to Start Point, including the Isles of Scilly. The main building along

The Scillonian III arriving at Penzance in May 1985.

the harbour road–the Buoy Store–is to become a museum of Trinity House and its lighthouses. Penzance has always been the mainland port for services to the Isles of Scilly. The 1,255 ton Scillonian III, built by Appledore Shipbuilders in 1977, currently maintains the daily passenger and cargo service to the islands.

NEWLYN

Newlyn was a medieval fishery and its original 15th century pier survives within the subsequently enlarged harbour. During the 18th and 19th centuries Newlyn expanded as a major fishery with pilchard seines, mackerel and herring fisheries, and the most important drift fleet in Cornwall. Between 1866 and 1873 the harbour and quays were extended. The North or Victoria Pier was built in 1888. Newlyn remains as Cornwall's major fishing port, under the management of the Newlyn Pier and Harbour Commissioners. A major expansion of fishing facilities, with a new pier built into the centre of the harbour, have recently been completed. These facilities are used not only by its own fleet, but also by trawlers from the east coast and the continent, although without the problems that arose in the past with the arrival of 'foreign' fishermen. In the Newlyn Riots of 1896 fighting broke out, when east coast fishermen went to sea on a Sunday, which could not be tolerated by the strict Methodist fishermen of the village.

For many years the South Pier has been reserved for the roadstone quarries at nearby Penlee Point; formerly the stone was transported onto the quay by a narrow gauge railway from the quarry.

MOUSEHOLE

An ancient fishing harbour which supported pilchard and mackerel fishing. Mousehole was the first harbour in the county to have a pier, which was built during the last decade of the 14th century, when it was the most important fishing place in the county. In 1849 over 800 people, including packers, curers and coopers were employed in the harbour's fishing trade, 425 being fishermen. The ancient pier was extended in 1840 and again in 1861 when a new pier was built. At the harbour entrance, as a protection in heavy weather, baulks of timber may be placed between the piers, to stop the sea breaking into the harbour. Until the 1970s a splendid timber crane stood on the south side of the entrance to handle these considerable baulks.

LAMORNA COVE

Once a fishing porth, extensive granite quarries were opened up, immediately above the cove, and the short pier was constructed in 1853-54 for the

Lamorna Cove.

export of stone. Substantial evidence survives in the shape of granite blocks, which litter the cove.

PENBERTH

As at other small coves in Penwith, a narrow and steep beach has been used for fishing over the centuries, but beaching boats must always have been a problem. Here, as at Porthgwarra, a large windlass or capstan was used to haul boats up above high tide level, but the example at Penberth has survived and been restored, thanks to the National Trust, who own the cove.

Penberth, with the beach windlass on the left.

PORTHCURNO

The first long distance telegraph cable, from Bombay, came ashore here, in 1870; the coves connections with the Cable & Wireless Co. continue to this day, with their extensive Engineering School.

SENNEN COVE

In 1850 there were 18 fishing vessels registered in Sennen, employing some 80 people. Pilchards represented the major catch, but the cove was also frequented by shoals of red mullet. The Round House at Sennen housed a capstan for pulling the boats up onto the beach. The pier was built in 1908 to offer protection to shipping and the lifeboat. Sennen has been a lifeboat station since 1853. This most westerly village in mainland England still maintains crab and lobster potting.

St.Ives Harbour.

ST.IVES TO NEWQUAY

ST.IVES

St.Ives' first stone pier was built for the protection of fishing vessels during the 15th century. An outer pier was designed by the noted engineer John Smeaton, and was completed in 1770. This pier was extended in 1888-90, but the original section remains, marked by the circular structure in the centre which used to be the lighthouse at what was the end of the pier. In 1864-67 an outer wooden pier was erected to help enclose the beach. This structure suffered from storm damage and only a short stone stump at the landward end now remains. The West Pier was built in 1894 for shipping roadstone from local quarries.

Tin and copper from the St.Just district was exported from St.Ives and the port had long attracted a general cargo trade. But St.Ives was primarily a fishing port, supporting both drift and seine fisheries. As the principal pilchard fishery in Cornwall, St.Ives became so busy that Acts of Parliament were necessary in 1776 and 1841 to regulate the fishery. The fishing trade peaked in the 1830s and '40s with the port catching an average 22 million pilchards per year. Huers were stationed at Carn Crowse, Porthminster Point and Carrack Gladden Point, both to direct the seines and to signal change over times of seines working alloted sections or 'stems'. In 1905 there were still

200 fishing vessels registered, but the trade was in decline. Seining was nearly over by the first World War, although seines were registered until 1920. The harbour is filled with pleasure craft today, but not entirely to the exclusion of fishing. The lifeboat station was established in 1840.

LELANT

Lelant was a port for the district from the early 14th century, but in more recent times the quays have been associated with the large scale industrial activities of neighbouring Hayle.

HAYLE

In 1710-20 two tin smelting houses were established in Hayle, importing south Wales coal for the smelting process. Copper smelting was also undertaken giving the name Copperhouse to a district to the east of the town. John Harvey established a foundry at the water's edge in 1779. A weir and floodgates were erected at the mouth of the creek to scour the channel alongside Harvey's coal quays. Here the foundry company built a 450 yards long wharf in 1819. The opposing Copperhouse Company built their own Copperhouse Quay adjoining it. Harveys' foundry became the most important in Cornwall employing, at times, 1000 men. The foundry manufactured mine engines and other mining equipment, but this declined after the 1860s with the closure of so many mines.

In 1831 Harveys established a steam packet service to Bristol, which in 1841 linked with the Great

Western Railway from London. In 1834 the Hayle Railway linked the Hayle quays to the mining district around Redruth. Having acquired their first small sloop in 1787, the fleet gradually increased, with some ships adapted to moving large steam engine parts for delivery from the foundry. They could then import coal and pig iron from south Wales for the foundry. It was hardly surprising that the Harveys then began shipbuilding, and after the launch of the *John Harvey* in 1834, one or two new vessels were built and added to the fleet each year, mostly schooners up to about 70ft in length. It was then an obvious move into iron shipbuilding, and some notable–and fast–paddle steamers were built for the Bristol Packet service. The most famous of these was the *Cornubia* of 1858, which was to be sold three years later to act as a successful blockade runner for the Confederate States of America. The largest vessel built at Hayle was the *Ramleh*, launched in 1891; but falling prices and competition from the larger up-country shipyards ended this branch of the business. The Harveys' Foundry itself closed in 1904.

There was a lifeboat stationed at Hayle from 1866 to 1920, and the maritime importance of the place was shown by its becoming a port of registry in its own right, albeit for a fairly short time.

The harbour entrance has never been easy, and dredging was required when sizable ships used the port. The electricity power station and small oil company depot were supplied by sea until the 1970s, and these formed the last regular cargoes. After the first and second World Wars, the metal scrap business of Thomas Ward used Hayle as a base for their business dismantling redundant warships, some of which were as large as battle-cruisers.

PORTREATH

An ancient fishing port, the harbour at Portreath was developed to serve the mining industry. The artificial harbour was built during the second half of the 18th century chiefly for trade with south Wales. The harbour was leased to Fox & Co. of Falmouth who improved facilities and built a new basin. An inner basin was constructed in 1846. In 1809 the Poldice tramroad, the first railway in Cornwall, was built, linking Portreath to the St.Day and Gwennap mining districts.

Fishing continued and a considerable general trade was attracted. D.W.Bain & Co. of Portreath maintained a fleet of trading schooners, numbering 16 vessels in 1880.

Many of the harbours of the north coast have difficult entrances, but none can match Portreath.

A ship had to make its way into the narrow entrance between the pier and a cliff face to the east. Then it had to negotiate the length of the channel up to the inner basin. No mean feat, particularly in the days of sail, when vessels often had to be warped up the channel. Trade declined considerably after the last war, and eventually ceased in the 1960s; the old quays, once piled high with ore and coal, were sold off for housing development.

ST.AGNES

There have been five attempts to construct an artificial harbour at St.Agnes. John Tonkin started in 1632 to construct a 'peer or key' to serve trading vessels. His efforts were destroyed in gales during the following winter. A second attempt, by Hugh Tonkin in 1684, was again destroyed by the sea. Hugh Tonkin's pier of 1699, built with the aid of Henry Winstanley, lasted until it was swept away by the sea in 1705. Thomas Tonkin completed the fourth harbour works in 1710. It was destroyed in 1736. In 1793 mining adventurers constructed a new harbour at the foot of the cliffs in Trevaunance Cove. Wooden staging on the cliffs above served as loading platforms, cargoes being lifted or lowered to the boats' holds by horse windlass. Ore was loaded by shute, similar to those at Porthoustock

M.T.Hitchens & Co. built schooners at St. Agnes and maintained their own fleet. There were also some local fishing boats. The harbour continued to function until the 1920s. Since then its piers have been washed away, apart from the foundation courses which can be seen at low tide below the cliff to the west, on the boulder strewn shore; this is all that remains as evidence of the harbour.

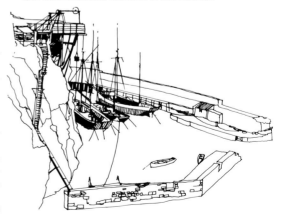

St. Agnes Harbour (Trevaunance Cove).

NEWQUAY

A stone pier existed in the 15th century for the convenience of ships prevented by weather from entering the River Gannel or Porth, either side of 'Newquay'. By the end of the 16th century the *new quay* was being built to replace the old pier, offering a harbour of refuge rather than trading facilities for what was no more than a small hamlet. Later, the local communities supported pilchard seines and curing cellars.

In 1833 Richard Lomax completed a harbour development which enclosed four acres. Five years later J T Austen (see Par) acquired the harbour and developed it for the export of minerals and china clay. In 1849 a railway linked Newquay to the clay district and Par Harbour.

Four shipyards built schooners, ketches etc. and Newquay became an important shipowning centre. About 150 trading vessels were owned at the peak of the harbour's activity. From the 1870's trade began to dwindle. The last outward cargo left the port in 1921. The final inward cargo—manure!—was landed by the schooner *Hobah*, in 1922.

The stone jetty in the centre of Newquay Harbour dates from 1870. The railway once emerged from a short tunnel in the cliffs, on a wooden bridge (now removed) and out on to the stone jetty (now isolated) in the middle of the harbour. Rails also ran onto the protecting outer pier. A second pier enclosed the harbour. By 1868 lodging houses for visitors already existed and the holiday trade has now been Newquay's major industry for many years.

Newquay Rowing Club have a number of pilot gigs, now used in the summer for racing. These include the *Newquay* built by Peters of St Mawes in 1812 and the *Dove* of 1820, as well as some built in the 1970s as a result of the welcome revival in gig racing.

On the cliff road, near the Atlantic Hotel, is the curious little Huer's House, a lookout for the seine fishery, where a watchman was stationed to spot the approaching pilchard shoals.

Huers House near Newquay.

PADSTOW & NORTH CORNWALL

PADSTOW

The tidal reaches of the River Camel provide the main estuarine haven on the northern coast of Cornwall. Located in the estuary is north Cornwall's largest port, Padstow. Padstow's first stone pier was built some time before 1536. Its site is now occupied by the large red brick warehouse of 1870, adjacent to North Quay; this splendid warehouse building is now under threat of destruction, in what would be a major act of vandalism.

The warehouse on North Quay, Padstow.

In the 16th century the port engaged in trade with Wales, Ireland and ports in the Bristol Channel. During the 17th and 18th centuries slate, tin and copper ore were exported. In the 19th century emigrant ships for Canada left from Padstow. In the early 20th century the port was used by herring fleets, to get their fish to Billingsgate via the London & South Western Railway at Padstow. China clay was exported, brought to the quayside from Wenford Bridge by the railway.

The port was a Customs base to counter smuggling. Customs officers, Preventive men and Coastguards were responsible for the immediate coastline. The original Customs House, together with a grain warehouse, are now converted as the Old Customs House Inn, on South Quay. The Customs and Excise offices are currently located in the former L&SWR station building of 1899. The fish sheds opposite were also built by the railway company. Sections of wooden awning and some British Rail notices are still in evidence on the shed building although the branch closed in 1966.

Six shipbuilding yards once occupied Padstow's foreshore. In the 19th century these were located

Padstow's old Customs House on the left and a warehouse building on the right, both now incorporated into The Old Customs House Inn.

at St.Georges Well (downstream from Padstow), Lower Yard (now North Quay waterside flats), North Jetty (on the red brick warehouse site), South Quay, Higher Yard (near the fish shed site) and Dennis Cove (where ships of 800 tons were built). During this period the port became active in ship management and deep sea trading. Padstow was for a time a shipowning community. In 1823 there were 27 registered shipowning ventures in the town.

The sand banks at the estuary mouth, and in particular the notorious Doom Bar, have restricted Padstow's growth as a major sea port. In 1829 the Padstow Harbour Association set up capstans on Stepper Point, at the mouth of the estuary, to improve navigation into the port by warping ships into the estuary against the elements. Remains of these capstans can still be seen. Owing to the dangerous coast and estuary mouth a lifeboat was established before 1825. In 1856 the R.N.L.I. assumed control of the station at Hawkers Cove, inside the mouth of the estuary. In 1967 the lifeboat station was moved to Mother Ivey's Bay on Trevose Head. A Land Rover, based in Padstow, takes the crew to the lifeboat, some three miles distant. A new Tyne class lifeboat was delivered in 1984.

Today a small fishing fleet is maintained. Sand is landed on the outer jetty of the large fish dock, which was built in 1910. A controversial flood prevention and sewage development is nearing completion at time of writing. The original scheme for a flood barrier has been extended to incorporate sewage improvements and create a floating yacht harbour. If finished as planned, the scheme will alter the nature of the harbour.

The Black Rock Ferry, which crosses the estuary from the ferry steps at the end of North or Ferry Jetty, is run by the Harbour Commissioners. This jetty was built in 1931 by a labour force drawn from the unemployed, during the Depression.

The outer quay of the Fish Dock at Padstow

WADEBRIDGE

Crumbling stone quays on either side of the River Camel, below the 15th century bridge, provide evidence of Wadebridge's past importance as a river port.

A fleet of tidal barges carried lime rich sand, dredged from the estuary, to farm hards above the bridge. The same barges also offered lighterage to schooners and ketches which drew too much water, fully ladened, to navigate the channel at Wadebridge.

From 1837 the Bodmin & Wadebridge Railway brought increased trade to the river quays. Granite from the DeLank Quarry on Bodmin Moor was exported. Stone for the present Eddystone Lighthouse (completed in 1882) left from these river quays. Slate, iron ore and china clay were also exported; coal, timber, limestone and general cargoes were imported.

The quays remained active until 1939. A few post war visits by small motor coasters failed to revive trade from the quays at Wadebridge.

The river quays viewed from the bridge at Waderbridge.

PORT QUIN

One of the three porths centred around Port Isaac, Port Quin was a small fishing village. Pilchard seines and shellfish pots were maintained. A limited beach trade brought in coal and manure–agricultural work being an alternative occupation for the villagers. The fish cellars still stand, but together with the stores and other cottages, have been converted for holiday accommodation.

Owned today by the National Trust, Port Quin is notable as a dead or deserted village. A degree of mystery surrounds its demise. Unfortunately, surviving records of the village lend themselves to differing interpretations. It can only be said, with any certainty, that the fishing fleet ceased to exist near the end of the 19th century and the population dwindled rapidly.

Port Quin.

PORT ISAAC

There was a pilchard fishery at Port Isaac before the 16th century. A protective stone pier was built during the Tudor period and its remains are still visible on the northern shore, inside the post-first World War breakwaters.

In 1850 there were 49 fishing boats registered and 4 fish cellars. The large fish cellars in the south corner of the cove were built in the 19th century and continue to be used by the fishing fleet. The sheds under the Pentus wall, in the northern corner of the cove, were built for storing fishing tackle. Roofing slate from the nearby Delabole Quarries was shipped out from the beach. There were two boat building yards in Port Isaac, adjacent to the fish cellars.

A small coasting trade developed from the slate shipping activity. Ketches and smacks of 50-80 tons were built and owned in Port Isaac and traded mainly in the Irish Sea.

The old lifeboat station, now the village post office, was established in 1869. The lifeboat had to be wheeled through the narrow streets on a carriage. A new station was opened in 1927, at the top of the beach and slipway. It was closed just six years later, but the substantial boathouse still stands. An inshore lifeboat was introduced in 1967. The lifeboat is housed inside the fish cellars.

Port Isaac. The low building on the right is the fish cellars.

PORT GAVERNE

A pilchard fishery during the Tudor period and for long the major slate shipping port for the Delabole quarries. Early in the 19th century the slate company built the 'Great Slate Road' to Port Gaverne. Wagons brought slate to a quayside, the remains of which are still discernable on the southern shore of the cove. The slate was stacked on the quayside and shipped out aboard schooners and ketches, which took the beach. A chain of people, mainly women, carried the slate to the boats, where it was packed between layers of hay.

There were four seine companies in the 19th century. Two of the cellars were at the head of the cove, while the other two were sited on the southern shore. These latter two survive, converted to holiday apartments, but clearly discernable as fish cellars. A house now called 'Chimneys', opposite the beach, was originally a salting house. Boat building yards at the head of the cove built trading and fishing vessels up to 50 tons.

TINTAGEL

Up to the 19th century roofing slate was exported from this unlikely location. From wooden staging, similar to that in use at Trevaunance Cove, tackle lowered slate to the beach below.

BOSCASTLE

A particularly spectacular and twisting entrance to this picturesque cove has rendered Boscastle a favourite of visitors to the north Cornwall coast. Despite commercialism at the landward end of the village, the waterfrontage along the harbour remains unspoilt, thanks largely to its ownership by the National Trust.

Boscastle, from an illustration by Charles Napier Hemy.

Boscastle's first pier was erected in the 16th century to protect the inner cove from the action of the sea. This pier was soon destroyed, but later in the century a second one was built and it is largely this structure which still stands on the southern shore. In 1740 it was extensively restored.

A fleet of trading vessels was maintained by the port, exporting manganese ore from mines near Launceston, during the early 19th century, and china clay from Bodmin moor later in the century. Other exports included slate, corn and bark.

A second breakwater projects into the narrow entrance from the northern shore, to help break the seas which rush into the ravine. However, in the event of bad weather, trading vessels left the quayside and took the ground of the harbour, held down by strong hawsers. These especially thick ropes were kept at Boscastle and made available by the Harbourmaster.

CRACKINGTON HAVEN

Evidence of a limited beach trade remains today in the shape of a small group of semi-derelict buildings at the top of the beach, which served as storehouses.

BUDE

Bude was primarily an agricultural trading port, serving farming communities remote from any other port or major centre of population . The idea for a canal to trade inland was first mooted in 1770. In 1819 two canals were approved, one to terminate near Launceston, the other near Holsworthy. Lime bearing sea sand was transported inland, the sand being dug from the beach at Bude. A 2ft gauge tramway, with man handled wagons, brought the sand to the canal quayside. Much of the tramway, near the lock gates in Bude, is still in location.

Incline planes instead of locks, linked different canal levels. Canal barges (in fact small 'tub boats') with wheels, engaged rails on the inclines. The power to lift the barges came from counter-balance water-weighted buckets in deep shafts, which were filled at the top and emptied at the bottom, once the barge had reached the summit.

At the entrance to the sea lock at Bude a protecting breakwater was built to safeguard shipping waiting to enter the canal. This was destroyed in 1828, but twelve years later the surviving breakwater was completed. Long mooring posts set into the sand near the breakwater acted as lead in marks at high tide. Schooners were sometimes lightered owing to lack of water at the sea lock. Trading vessels transshipped cargoes onto the quay or into barges at the wharf alongside the broad reach of the canal inside the sea lock at Bude. It was originally hoped that this navigation might link with a similar venture on the River Tamar. But in the event, only the Tamar Manure Navigation at Gunnislake was completed in the southern scheme. After the railway arrived in Launceston, Holsworthy and then Bude itself, trade on the canal declined. In 1891 an Act was sought to abandon sections. In 1901 Bude-Stratton Urban District Council purchased the section of the canal at the Bude end for waterworks improvements. A mile or so of canal survives inland from Bude, but much of the upper parts of the canal can be traced. In Bude the canalside quays are used for leisure purposes. A museum is housed in a canalside warehouse.

The canal transformed Bude into a stronghold of small ship ownership. Bude's maritime trade supported shipbuilding, shipowning, shipping agents, chandlers, merchants and banking. Bude's isolated location, the community's involvement in shipowning and the sea lock and canal basin extended the port's maritime trade long after the canal proper had closed.

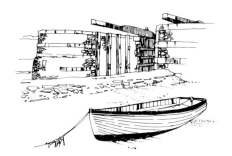

The Bude Canal sea lock

FURTHER READING

Bainbridge, G.	The Wooden Ships & Iron Men (Charlestown Estate Ltd. 1980)
Barton, R.M.	A History of the Cornish China Clay Industry (Bradford Barton 1966)
Drew, J.H.	Rail & Sail to Pentewan (Twelveheads Press 1986)
Greenhill, B.	The Merchant Schooners (Conway Maritime Press 1988)
Greenhill & Slade	Westcountry Coasting Ketches (Conway Maritime Press 1974)
Harris, K.	Hevva: Cornish Fishing in the Days of Sail (Dyllansow Truran 1983)
Kittridge, A.	Passenger Steamers of the River Fal (Twelveheads Press 1988)
Kittridge, A.	Passenger Steamers of the River Tamar (Twelveheads Press 1984)
Langley & Small	Estuary & River Ferries of South West England.(Waine Research Publications 1984)
Merry, I.D.	The Shipping & Trade of the River Tamar [2 parts] (National Maritime Museum 1980)
Noall, C.	The Story of Cornwall's Ports & Harbours (Tor Mark Press 1970)
Oliver, A.S.	Boats & Boatbuilders in West Cornwall (Bradford Barton 1971)
Pearse, R.	The Ports & Harbours of Cornwall (H.E.Warne 1963)
Ward Jackson, C.H.	Ships & Shipbuilders of a West Country Seaport–Fowey 1786-1939 (Twelveheads Press 1987)
Winstanley, M.	The Story of Port Isaac, Port Quin & Port Gaverne (Lodenek Press 1984)

The Royal Albert Bridge and Saltash Town Quay on the River Tamar. At the quay are the steamers Prince and Alexandra (outside). The Industrial Training Ship Mt. Edgcumbe is moored offshore.

Front cover: **The port of Looe.** *Michael Messenger.*

ISBN 0 906294 15 0   © Alan Kittridge 1989, 1991
First published 1989. Second impression, with minor ammendments 1991.
Twelveheads Press. Chy Mengleth, Twelveheads, Truro, Cornwall TR4 8SN.